JN265422

THE BEST OF
JAPANESE CULTURE

日本風物詩

装幀/*Cover Design*
PARK. Sutherland Inc.

写真/*Photographs*
Katsuhiko Mizuno
p.21, p.29, p.31上, p.65, p.117

Stuart Varnam-Atkin
p.43, p.51, p.57下, p.59, p.61, p.63, p.91, p.97

Mitsuo Tsukada
p.19, p.25, p.27, p.33, p.35, p.39上, p.45, p.55, p.73下, p.105, p.135, p.145, p.181

浅草寺 p.31下
毎日新聞社/アフロ p.111
Universal Images Group/アフロ p.113
AP/アフロ p.183

photolibrary, PIXTA, MIXA, 素材辞典, IBC編集部

THE BEST OF JAPANESE CULTURE
日本風物詩

ステュウット ヴァーナム-アットキン=著
Stuart Varnam-Atkin

とよざきようこ=訳
Translated by Yoko Toyozaki

IBCパブリッシング

Introduction

Why 108?
What's *igo*?
What are *ema*?
What are *kokeshi*?
What does 7-5-3 mean?
Why do brides wear white?
What are food samples made of?
Why do O-jizo statues carry a staff?
Why are noodles eaten on December 31st?
How many beads are there on a Buddhist rosary?

As we move ever closer to the excitement of the 2020 Olympic Games in Tokyo, interest in Japan and its culture is growing rapidly worldwide, and more and more foreign visitors are arriving to experience Japanese culture in person. Some are passionate about the latest trends, such as 'maid cafes' and anime. Others can't wait to see the famous sights of Kyoto and Nara, the ancient capital cities.

まえがき

108って？
囲碁ってなに？
絵馬は何ですか？
こけしとはなんのこと？
七五三とはなんですか？
花嫁はなぜ白い衣装を着るの？
食品サンプルは何からつくるの？
お地蔵さまはなぜ錫杖を持って歩く？
そばを大晦日に食べるのはなぜですか？
仏教徒の数珠に珠はいくつ並んでいるのか？

　2020年東京オリンピックのわくわくするような大イベントに向かう今、世界中で日本や日本文化への関心度が急速に高まっており、その文化をじかに体験しようと来日する観光客がますます増えている。メイドカフェやアニメのような最新トレンドに夢中な人もいれば、奈良や京都など古都の観光地訪問が待ちきれない人もいるだろう。だがその人たちのだれもが同じように感じることがある。それは、膨大な季節の風物詩と共に、

But one thing they all tend to feel is the wonderful way in which the ultra-modern co-exists with many elements of traditional Japan, along with a whole host of seasonal attractions.

By presenting a broad selection of colorful aspects of Japanese culture that can still be seen all over the country today, this bilingual book tries to answer some of the mountain of questions that foreigners tend to ask. It includes not only short explanations of each item, but also carefully selected photographs that will give a vivid visual idea of Japanese life to those who have never experienced it, as well as providing fond memories for those who have been lucky enough to visit Japan.

Japanese terms are distinguished by italics the first time they appear in each item. I hope you find the text interesting and the photos a pleasure to look at. My thanks go to Kyoko Kagawa and Hiromi Hishiki for their enthusiasm and support, and Yoko Toyozaki for her painstaking translation.

Stuart Varnam-Atkin
Tokyo, 2014

超現代的な側面が、伝統的な要素の数々と見事に共存している日本の姿である。

　今日でも全国津々浦々に見られる色彩豊かな日本文化のあれこれを幅広くとりあげた本書は、外国人が疑問をもつ山ほどの不思議のいくつかにバイリンガルで答えようとするものだ。それぞれのテーマに関する短い説明や慎重に選ばれた写真によって、日本の日常を垣間見たことがない人たちにはそのイメージが鮮明になり、一方で、訪日を果たされた幸運な人たちには懐かしい思い出がよみがえってくることだろう。

　日本語は、それぞれのテーマで初めて出現する場合、斜体で記してそれが日本語であることが分かるようにした。読者が本書の内容や掲載された写真に興味を持ち楽しんでくだされば幸いである。編集者の賀川京子さん、菱木啓美さんの熱意とご支持に、そして豊崎洋子さんのていねいな翻訳に感謝の意を表する。

　　　　　　　　　　　　　　　　　　ステュウット ヴァーナム−アットキン
　　　　　　　　　　　　　　　　　　2014年　東京にて

目次

Introduction　まえがき　*4*

Chapter 1
寺社仏閣　*Shrines & Temples*　*15*

Jinja　神社　*16*

Shimenawa　しめ縄　*18*

Torii　鳥居　*20*

Komainu　狛犬　*24*

Saisenbako　賽銭箱　*26*

Kemari　蹴鞠　*28*

Tera　寺　*30*

Goju-no-to　五重塔　*32*

Kane　鐘　*34*

Ema　絵馬　*38*

O-mikuji　おみくじ　*40*

O-mamori　お守り　*42*

O-jizo-sama　お地蔵さま　*44*

Chapter 2

街の風景 *Out & About* 47

Koban 交番 *48*

Maneki-neko 招き猫 *50*

Noren のれん *52*

Nawa-noren 縄のれん *54*

Chochin 提灯 *56*

Shokuhin sanpuru 食品サンプル *58*

Daruma だるま *60*

Kokeshi こけし *62*

Maiko 舞妓 *64*

Chapter 3

冠婚葬祭 *Ceremonial Occasions & Items* 67

Shinzen-kekkonshiki 神前結婚式 *68*

Tsuno-kakushi 角隠し *70*

Shio 塩 *72*

Juzu 数珠 *74*

Mokugyo 木魚 *76*

Mizuhiki　水引　*78*

Noshi　のし　*80*

Chapter 4

遊び　*Games*　*83*

Shogi　将棋　*84*

Go　碁　*86*

Hanetsuki　羽根つき　*88*

Koma　コマ　*90*

Tako　たこ　*92*

Sugoroku　すごろく　*94*

Karuta　かるた　*96*

Hanafuda　花札　*98*

Uta-garuta　歌がるた　*100*

Chapter 5

伝統芸能・美術　*Features of Traditional Life*　*103*

Men　面　*104*

Noh 能 *106*

Kyogen 狂言 *108*

Bunraku 文楽 *110*

Ukiyo-e 浮世絵 *112*

Niwa 庭 *116*

Bonsai 盆栽 *118*

Kakejiku 掛け軸 *120*

Ikebana 生け花 *122*

Shiro 城 *124*

Tenshukaku 天守閣 *126*

Chapter 6

歳時記 *Seasonal Features* *129*

春 SPRING

Momo-no-sekku 桃の節句 *130*

Hina-ningyo ひな人形 *132*

Hanami 花見 *134*

Koinobori こいのぼり *136*

Gogatsu-ningyo 五月人形 *138*

夏 SUMMER

Tanabata-kazari　七夕飾り　*140*

Hanabi　花火　*142*

Mikoshi　神輿　*144*

Bon-kazari　盆飾り　*146*

Sensu　扇子　*148*

Uchiwa　うちわ　*150*

Sudare & Yoshizu　すだれ／よしず　*152*

Kakigori　かき氷　*154*

Kaya　蚊帳　*156*

Katori-senko　蚊取り線香　*158*

Furin　風鈴　*160*

秋 AUTUMN

Momiji-gari　紅葉狩り　*162*

Tsukimi　月見　*164*

Shichi-go-san　七五三　*166*

Chitose-ame　千歳飴　*168*

Botamochi & Ohagi　ぼたもち（おはぎ）　*170*

冬 WINTER

Kadomatsu　門松　*172*

Shime-kazari　しめ飾り　*174*

Mochitsuki　もちつき　*176*

Kagami-mochi　鏡もち　*178*

Toshikoshi-soba　年越しそば　*180*

Joya-no-kane　除夜の鐘　*182*

Hatsu-mode　初詣　*184*

Hamaya　破魔矢　*186*

O-toso　おとそ　*188*

O-toshidama　お年玉　*190*

O-sechi-ryori　おせち料理　*192*

Kamakura　かまくら　*194*

Chapter 1

寺社仏閣

Shrines & Temples

Jinja 神社

Normal Shinto shrines connected with ancestor worship are called *jinja*, often including the suffix *–miya* in the name. However, several other names are used, depending on the status and history of the shrine. *Taisha* is a very sacred name, as in Izumo Taisha in Shimane Prefecture. High-ranked shrines closely connected with an emperor or enshrining a past emperor are called *jingu*, as in Meiji Jingu in Tokyo and Ise Jingu in Mie Prefecture. The suffix *-gu* also suggests Imperial family connections, as in Tsurugaoka Hachimangu in Kamakura.

　先祖崇拝と結びついた一般的な神道の社は神社と呼ばれ、たいていは名前の末尾に「宮」がつく。だが、神社の社格と沿革に応じてさまざまな社号がある。島根県の出雲大社にあるような大社は非常に神聖な社号である。東京の明治神宮や三重県の伊勢神宮のように、天皇とのつながりが深かったり、昔の天皇を祭ってある社格の高い神社は神宮と呼ばれる。鎌倉の鶴岡八幡宮のように、末尾に「宮」がつく神社も皇室とのつながりを示している。

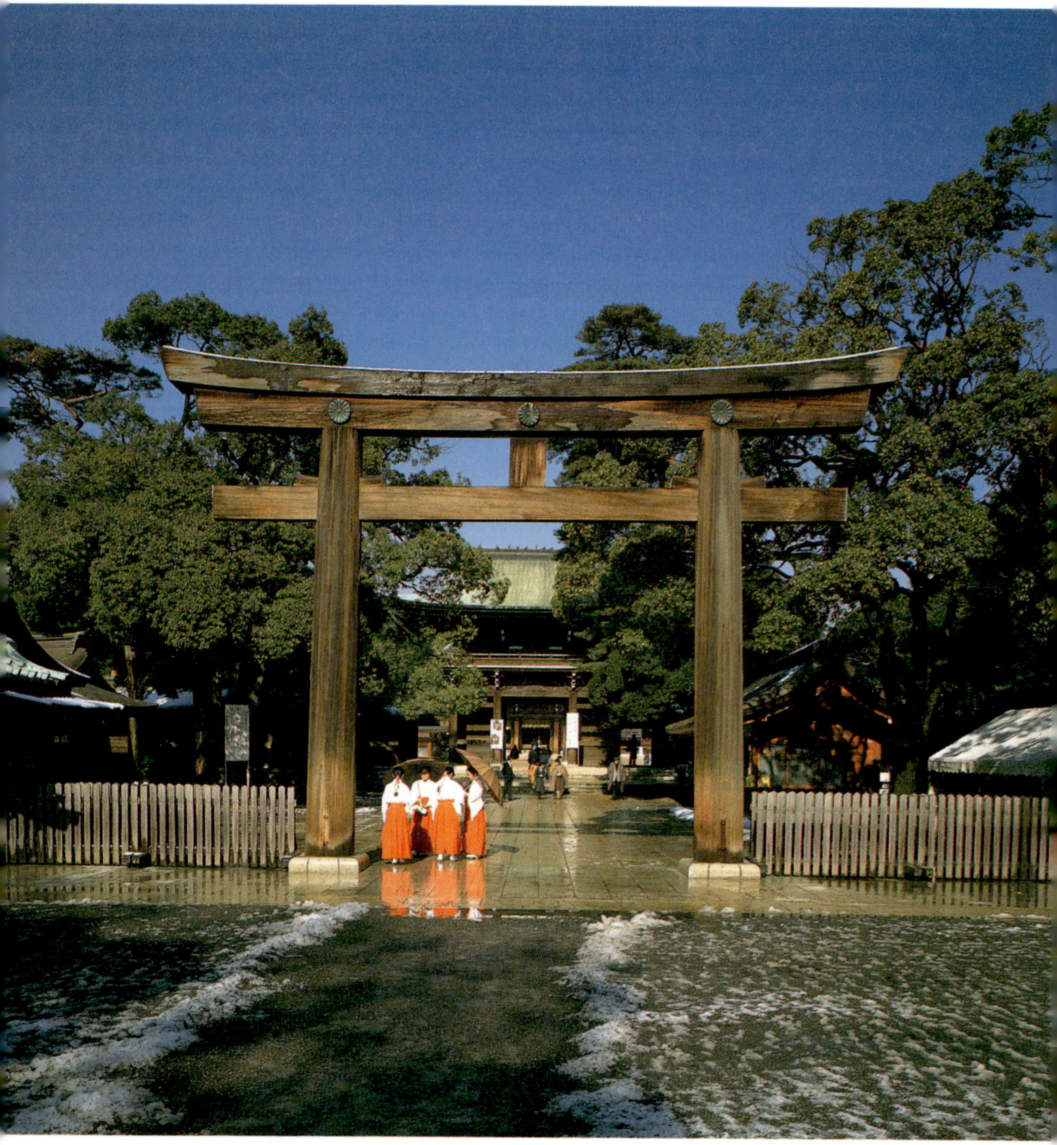

Shimenawa しめ縄

At the entrance and elsewhere in the shrine grounds, you will see *shimenawa* twisted straw ropes from which hang strips of white paper (*shide*). They indicate the edge of a sacred place and are sometimes hung around sacred trees and rocks.

The approach to a shrine is indicated by at least one *torii* symbolic gateway. Like the roofed lychgate of an old English church, the first torii marks the border between the everyday and sacred worlds. The number of torii is not fixed. You should pass through them to cleanse your heart and mind ready to appear before the enshrined god or gods. Always keep to the side of the path leading to the shrine as the center is reserved for the deities.

神社の入り口など、境内では、細長く切った白い紙（四手）が垂れ下がるしめ縄というねじったわらのロープを目にすることだろう。これは神聖な場所の境界を示すもので、神木や岩にかけられることもある。

神社の参道には、門を象徴する鳥居が少なくとも1基はある。イギリスの古い教会の墓地の入口にある屋根付きの門のように、一の鳥居は俗界と聖域の境界を示している。鳥居の数は決まっていない。参拝者はこの鳥居をくぐって心を清め、祭られている神の前に立つ準備を整える。参道の中央は神さまのために用意されたものなので、常に端を歩くよう努める。

19

寺社仏閣

Torii 鳥居

Torii have been described as one of the finest artistic creations formed by just four intersecting lines. The characters for 'torii' literally mean 'bird-perch.' Neither the origin of the name or the design is clear. Like the English word 'door', the name may be derived from the old Indian word *torana*, meaning 'gate.' Torii closely resemble gateways found in China and Korea, but they may simply have developed from ancient gateways similar to the *mon* gateways still found in front of old houses and temple precincts.

　鳥居は、たった4本の線が交差して形成される最も見事な芸術品の1つといわれてきた。「鳥居」という漢字には、文字どおり「鳥のとまり木」という意味があるが、その呼称や形の起源ははっきりしない。英語のdoorと同じように、鳥居は門を意味するインドの昔の言葉toranaを起源にするとの説がある。中国や韓国で見られる門にもよく似ているが、今でも旧家や古寺で見かけるような古い時代の門構えが単に発展しただけなのかもしれない。

21

寺社仏閣

Torii are constructed of *hinoki* (cypress) wood, stone, metal or concrete. There are more than a dozen main design variations, most of them with two posts (*hashira*), a top lintel (*kasagi*) and a tie-beam (*nuki*) connecting the posts. They range from the colossal, stark modern steel 1st Torii at Yasukuni Jinja in Tokyo, with its straight *shimmei*-style kasagi and nuki, to the famous and more elaborate red *ryobu*-style torii at Itsukushima Shrine at Miyajima, near Hiroshima, which stands in the sea. Fushimi Inari Shrine in Kyoto has tunnels formed by thousands of red torii. In the case of Tsurugaoka Hachimangu in Kamakura, the three torii are a great distance apart because many worshippers came by ship and walked from the beach.

鳥居の建築には、ヒノキや石、金属、コンクリートなどが使用される。ほとんどが2本の柱と1本の笠木、そして1本の貫からなり、主なものでも10数種を超える形式がある。そのバリエーションは、東京、靖国神社の巨大で堅牢な鋼管製の大鳥居に代表される直線的な神明鳥居から、広島の宮島、厳島神社で有名な、より装飾的な朱塗りの両部鳥居まで、さまざまである。この厳島神社の鳥居は海の中に立っている。京都の伏見稲荷大社には、何千もの朱塗りの鳥居が連なったトンネルがある。鎌倉の鶴岡八幡宮の場合、3基ある鳥居の間にかなりの距離がある。これは船で来て浜辺から歩いた参拝者が多かったからだ。

寺社仏閣

Komainu　狛犬

At each side of the entrance to a shrine there are often two stone, wooden or bronze statues of mythical guardian beasts resembling lions. Called *komainu*, they ward off evil. In the case of Inari shrines dedicated to the god of the harvest and industry, the statues are of foxes. The pathways to the shrine are lined by *toro* stone lanterns, usually donated by devotees. Near the shrine buildings there is a roofed water trough (*chozuya* or *temizuya*) where you wash your hands and rinse out your mouth using one of the ladles (*hishaku*) provided. Note that you should not drink from the ladle but pour water into your cupped hand.

　神社入り口の両脇には、石製や木造、あるいは銅製の獅子に似た想像上の守護獣の像が一対で置かれていることが多い。狛犬と呼ばれ、魔除けとなる。豊穣と商いの神を祭る稲荷神社の場合は、キツネの像が置かれる。神社の参道に並ぶ石製の灯篭は、一般的に信者が献納したものだ。社殿の近くには屋根つきの水槽（手水舎＝「ちょうずや」または「てみずや」）があって、参拝者は備えてあるひしゃくを使ってここで手を洗い口をすすぐ。留意すべきは、ひしゃくからじかに飲むのではなく、すぼめた手に水を注いで飲むことである。

寺社仏閣

Saisenbako 賽銭箱

Shrine buildings tend to be simple in appearance, often undecorated. They are designed for worshipping the gods, not for preaching by priests. The main buildings are the *Haiden* Outer Hall or Oratory for public worship and the *Honden* Inner Sanctuary, which contains symbolic objects of worship and is out of bounds to the general public. In front of the Haiden there is always a money box for offerings (*saisenbako*) and a rope with small bells hanging from the roof. You throw in some money (usually coins), pull the rope, clap twice to attract the attention of the gods and then pray with your hands lifted to face level.

　社殿は外観が質素なものが多く、装飾のないものも珍しくない。神を拝むための場所であって、神職が教えを説くための場所ではない。中核となる社殿は、参拝者の拝礼のために設けた前殿である拝殿と、聖域である本殿である。本殿にはご神体が納められており、一般参拝者の本殿への立ち入りは許されていない。拝殿の正面には必ず献金を受ける箱（賽銭箱）があり、小さな鈴がついた縄が屋根から垂れ下がっている。賽銭箱に現金（ふつうは小銭）を投げ入れ、縄を引っ張り、神々の注意を引くために二度かしわ手を打つ。それから両手を顔の高さで合わせ、祈りを捧げる。

27

寺社仏閣

Kemari 蹴鞠

The ancient non-competitive amusement called *kemari* (or *shukiku*) proves that there have long been Asians skilled at keeping a ball in the air with their feet. Probably introduced to Japan from China in the 7th century, it can still be seen at several shrines, such as Shimogamo Jinja in Kyoto, where it is played as a prayer for peace and a good harvest to kick off the New Year. The circle of usually eight players (*mariashi*) wearing ancient court costumes and leather shoes shout "Ari", "Ya" and "Oh" as they kick a 24-centimeter-diameter deerskin ball (*mari*) to each other, trying to please the deities by keeping it in the air as long as possible. They can use any part of their body apart from their hands and arms. The 2014 event at Shimogamo Jinja also featured an official World Cup match ball.

　勝負を競わない古代の遊戯、蹴鞠（「しゅうきく」とも読む）は、アジア人が古くからボールを落とさずに蹴り続ける技に優れていたことを立証するものだ。おそらくは7世紀に中国から渡来したもので、今日でも蹴鞠を行う神社がある。例えば、京都の下賀茂神社では、年の初めにその年の平穏と豊作を祈願して蹴鞠はじめが行われる。通常は平安装束に身を包み革製の靴をはいた鞠足と呼ばれる8人の競技者が輪になって、「アリ」「ヤア」「オウ」などと掛け声を発しながら、直径24センチの鹿皮製の鞠を蹴り合い、できるだけ長く蹴り続けて神々を楽しませる遊びである。競技者は、手と腕以外は体のどの部分を使ってもよい。下賀茂神社で行われた2014年の蹴鞠はじめでは、サッカーワールドカップ公式球も使われた。

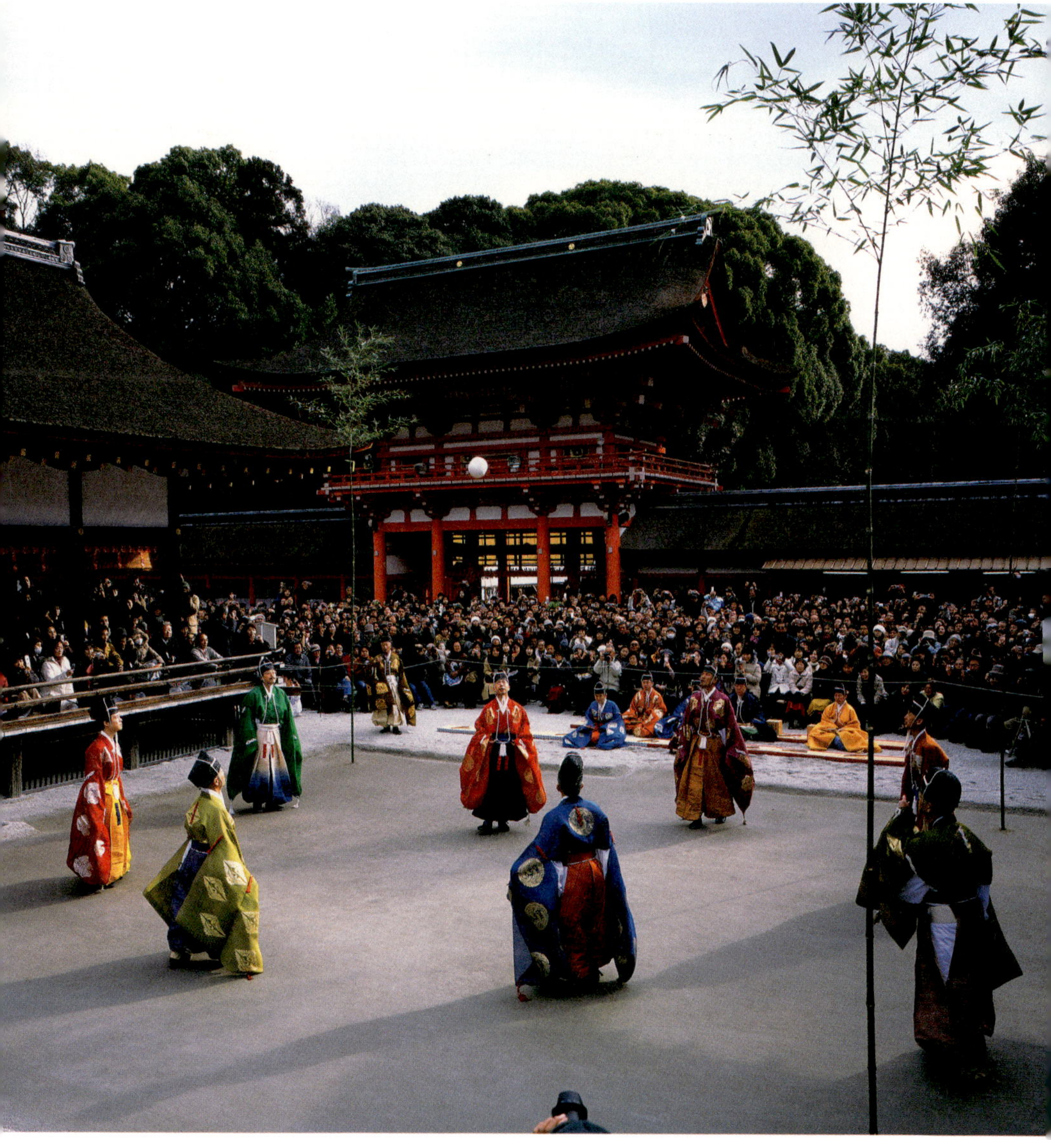

Tera 寺

Tera is the general term for a Buddhist temple. Temple names generally end in *-ji* (Sensoji in Tokyo, Todaiji in Nara) or *-in* (Chion-in in Kyoto). Up to the 19th century, shrines and temples were often combined, and architectural features of both can sometimes be found in the same location, such as the five-story pagoda in Itsukushima Shrine on the island of Miyajima. However, temples are distinguished by more flamboyant designs than Shinto shrines, and many sacred objects such as statues, bell towers, and pagodas.

　寺は仏教寺院を指す一般用語。寺院の名称はふつう「寺」(東京の浅草寺、奈良の東大寺) や「院」(京都の知恩院) で終わる。19世紀まで、神社と寺院はしばしば折衷・融合していたので、例えば、厳島神社に建つ五重塔のように、それぞれの建築上の特徴を備えたものが同じ敷地内に見受けられることもある。しかし寺は神社に比べて華やかなデザインが特徴で、たとえば仏像、鐘楼、塔などの神聖な物体がたくさんある。

31

寺社仏閣

Goju-no-to 五重塔

The design and names of temple buildings vary according to the sect. Most large temples have an impressive *Sanmon* main gate, a *Kondo* (also called *Hondo* or *Butsuden*) Main Hall, in which statues are kept, and a *Kodo* (or *Hatto*) Lecture Hall, where Buddhist scriptures are read. The other distinctive temple structure is the pagoda, often with five stories (*goju-no-to*). Like the India *stupa* from which their design evolved, pagodas hold holy relics. Recent research has proved that goju-no-to, supported by a central pillar, are remarkably earthquake-resistant.

寺の建物の設計および名称は宗派によって異なる。たいていの大寺院は、印象的な正門である山門（または三門）と、本尊を安置する金堂（本堂、仏殿）、仏典が読み上げられる講堂（法堂）を備える。ほかに、寺特有の建築物としては仏塔があり、五重塔と呼ぶ5層建てのものが多い。仏塔は、そのデザインの起源となるインドのストゥーパ（卒塔婆）と同じく、神聖な遺物を納めている。最近の研究から、心柱が支える五重塔は耐震性にも非常に優れていることがわかっている。

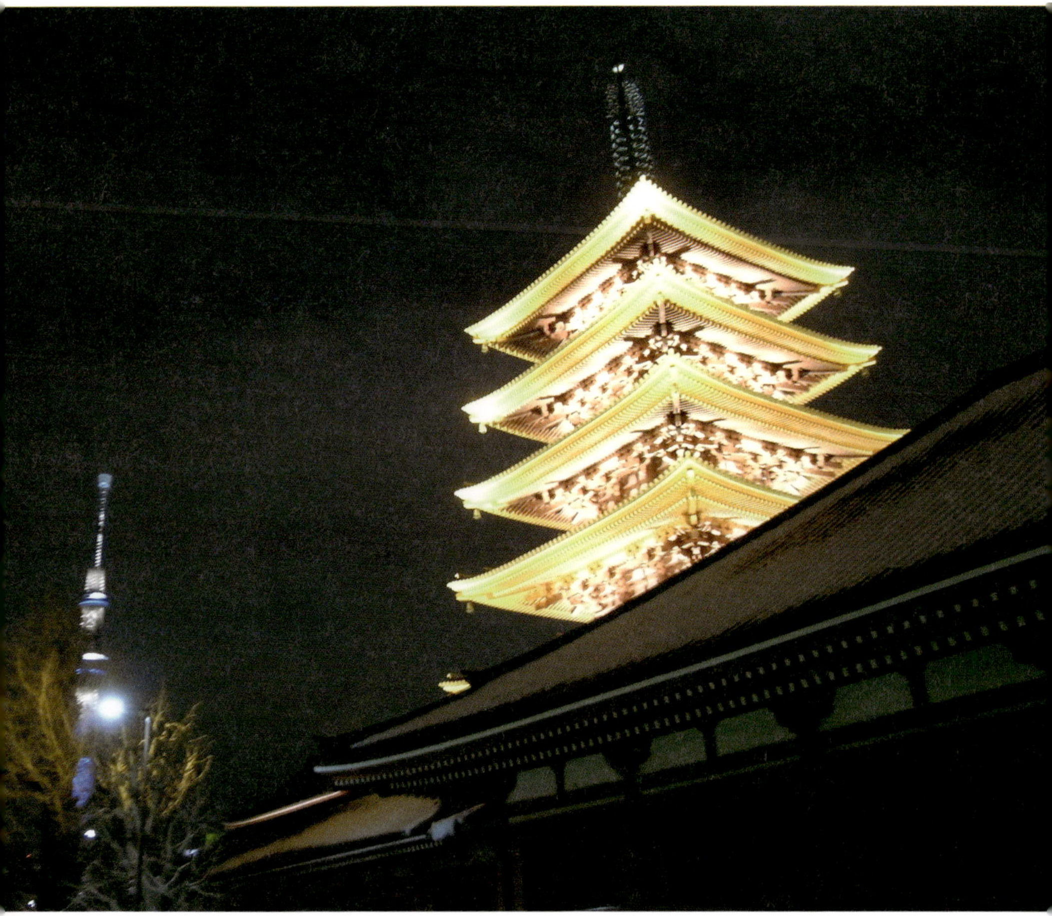

Kane 鐘

A hanging bell is called a *tsuri-gane* and temple bells are known as *bonsho*. However, technically speaking, bonsho are not 'bells' at all, but gongs; they are not rung by a swinging clapper but by a direct hit from the outside by a suspended wooden beam (*shumoku*). This is sometimes so large that it needs several people to swing it. Bonsho are housed in a special roofed belfry called a *shoro* (or *kane-tsuki-do*), separate from the main temple buildings.

つるした鐘は釣り鐘と呼ばれ、寺院にあるものは梵鐘として知られる。しかし厳密にいうと、梵鐘は「鐘」ではなく銅鑼である。内部にある舌を揺らすのではなく、外側につり下がっている木の棒（撞木）で直接ついて音を出す。撞木には非常に大きなものもあり、つくのに数人の手がかかることもある。梵鐘は鐘楼（あるいは鐘つき堂）と呼ばれる、特別な屋根つきの建物の中に設置され、本殿とは離れたところにある。

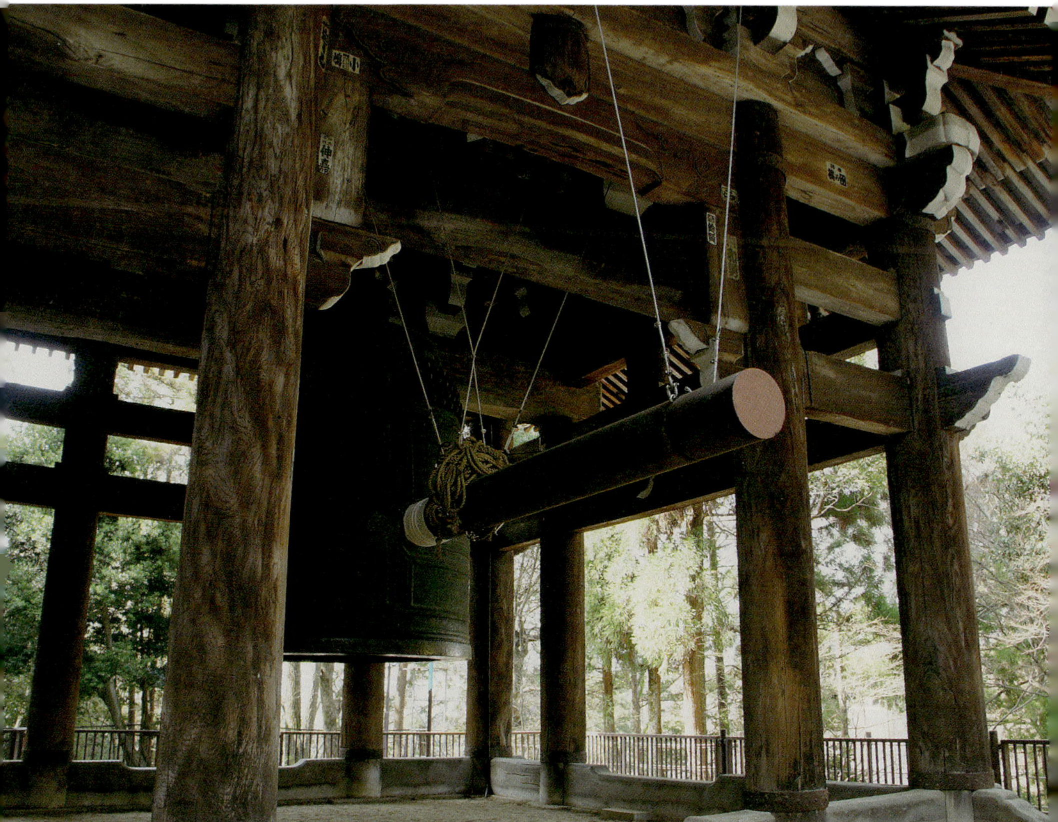

In the past, major temple bells were rung 108 times every morning and evening. Sometimes they also marked the time; the bell at Zojoji Temple in Edo (Tokyo) was rung every afternoon to call the mendicant monks back to the temple. In the quieter days of the past, it was said some bells could be heard dozens of kilometers away. Edo had more than 300 large temple bells at one time.

昔は大きな寺院の鐘は毎日、朝方と夕方に108回鳴らされていた。時刻を告げるためでもあった。例えば、江戸（今の東京）の増上寺の鐘はいつも午後の決まった時間に鳴らされ、托鉢に出ていた僧たちはそれを聞いて寺院に戻ってきたそうだ。静かだった昔は、鐘の音が数10キロ先まで届くこともあったという。江戸には一時期300を超える大きな梵鐘があった。

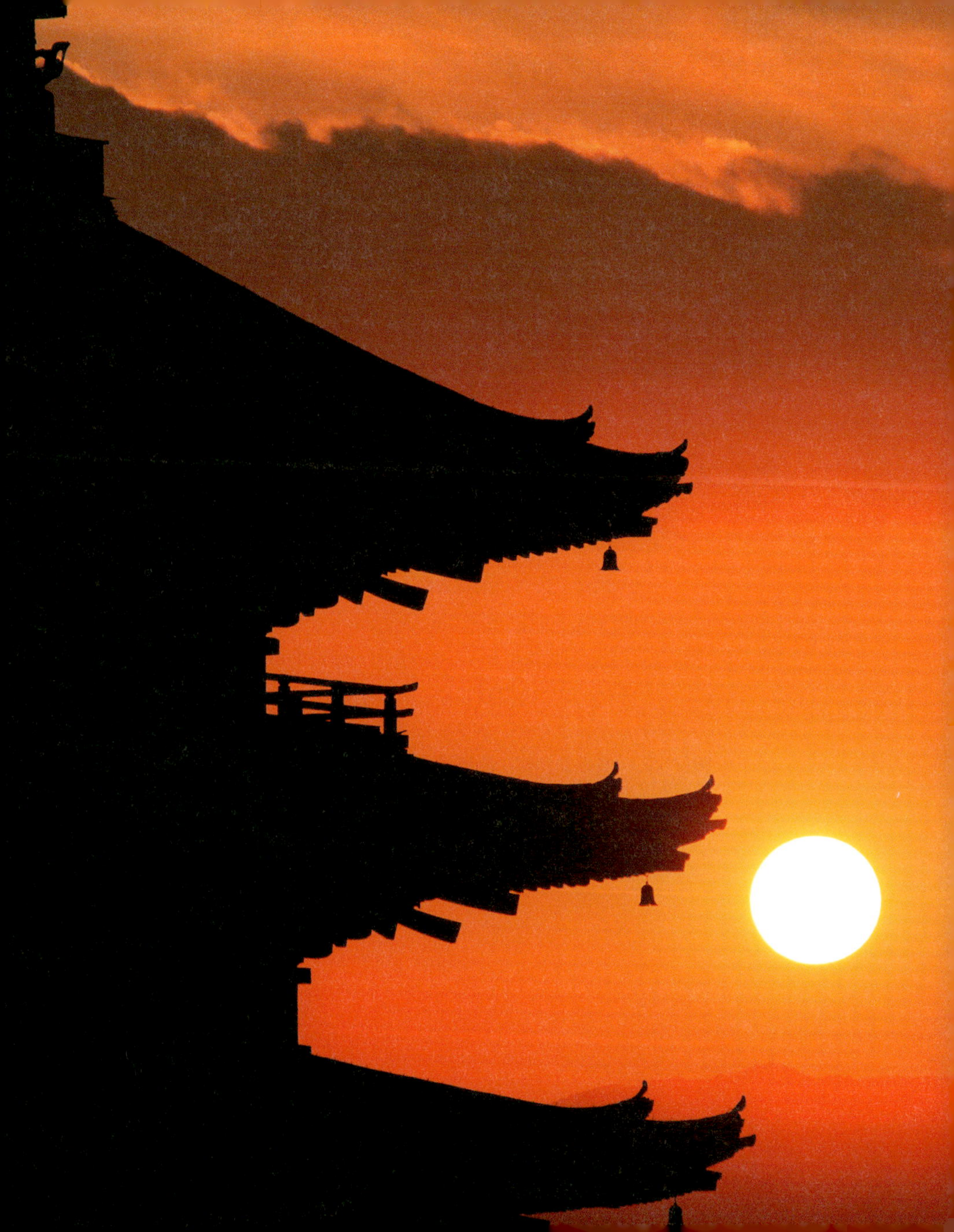

Ema　絵馬

Ema are small votive wooden tablets on sale at shrines. They are usually around 15 cms wide and five-sided like a cross-section of a house, often with a little roof at the top and cords attached for hanging. You write a wish on one and leave it at the shrine. Ema were originally offered as gratitude to the gods, but today they are more often used for making wishes. Thousands of ema bearing wishes for examination success can be seen at shrines dedicated to education. There are also large ema available for group wishes.

　絵馬とは木製の小型の奉納額で、境内で販売されている。幅およそ15センチ、家の横断面のような五角形で、上部に小さな屋根や、つるすためのひもがついていることが多い。願いを書いて神社に奉納する。もともとは神々に対する感謝の念を奉納した絵馬だが、今では祈願のために使われることが多い。学問の神が祭られている神社には、合格祈願の絵馬がたくさん見受けられる。大人数でまとめて祈願するための大型の絵馬もある。

39

寺社仏閣

O-mikuji おみくじ

O-mikuji (divine fortune) are written fortunes available at both shrines and temples for a small fee. The normal process is to pull or shake a bamboo stick out of a cylinder or a box. It's marked with a number and a priest or shrine maiden (*miko*) will hand you the corresponding paper that explains your fortune. However, there are now many o-mikuji vending machines that look rather like red mail boxes.

　おみくじ（神の占い）とは吉凶を記したもので、神社仏閣どちらでも、わずかなお金で求めることができる。筒や箱の中から引いたり振ったりして竹の棒を1本出すのが通常のやり方だ。棒には番号が記されており、神主か巫女が、その番号に該当する運勢が書かれた紙を手渡してくれる。しかし今では、赤い郵便ポストそっくりのおみくじ自動販売機が多くなっている。

寺社仏閣

O-mamori お守り

The word *mamori* means 'defence or protection,' and an *o-mamori* (or *mayoke*) is a kind of small talisman or amulet from a shrine or a temple to bring good luck and ward off evil. It consists of a piece of paper, wood or cloth blessed by a priest. It bears the name of the god and a prayer and is enclosed in a small brocade bag bearing the name of the shrine or temple. O-mamori generally have a specific application: to provide safety from traffic accidents; protection from illness; safe childbirth; success in examinations; etc. They can be carried around or hung somewhere, such as on a car dashboard. They are sometimes given as presents when someone returns from a visit to a famous shrine or temple.

「守り」とは「防衛・保護」を意味する言葉で、お守り（もしくは魔除け）は寺社で入手できる小型のタリスマン（幸運を呼ぶお守り）やアミュレット（魔除けのお守り）のようなもので、福を招いて厄をはらう。お守りには、僧侶や神主によって清められた紙や木や布などが入っている。そこには神の名前や祈禱文句が書いてあり、社寺の名前が入った小さな金襴織りの袋に封入されている。お守りにはふつう、交通安全や無病息災、安産祈願、入試合格など、特定の目的があり、持ち歩いたり、車のダッシュボードなどにつるすことができる。有名な神社や寺を訪ねた人がお土産にお守りをくれることもある。

43

寺社仏閣

O-jizo-sama　お地蔵さま

The stone *o-jizo-sama* statues standing all over Japan portray Jizo Bosatsu, the Buddhist savior believed to relieve people from all kinds of suffering. He is the guardian deity of travelers and pregnant women, and protects deceased children from demons. He appears as a monk with a shaved head wearing pilgrim's sandals, and there is the faintest of smiles on his face. In his left hand is a mystic jewel that grants wishes (*hoju*), and in his right hand a staff (*shakujo*) with six metal rings; pilgrims would jingle these as they walked along so that living creatures could hear them coming and get out of the way unharmed.

Local people often hang some item of clothing, such as a bib, around the statue's neck or shoulders and put a knitted hat or hood on his head.

　石像のお地蔵さまは日本中で見られる。お地蔵さまは仏教の救済者である地蔵菩薩を表現したもので、人々が抱えるあらゆる苦悩をとり除いてくれると信じられている。旅人や妊婦の守護聖人であり、死亡した子供を地獄の鬼から守る。坊主頭でわらじをはいた僧の姿で、その顔にはかすかに笑みをたたえている。左手には願いをかなえる神秘的な宝の珠（宝珠）を、右手には6個の金属環がついた杖（錫杖）を持つ。巡礼者たちは、生き物たちがその音を聞き脇によけて傷つかないよう、道中、この杖を鳴らして歩いた。
　近隣の人たちが地蔵の首や肩によだれかけのようなものをかけたり、頭に毛糸の帽子やずきんをかぶせたりすることがよくある。

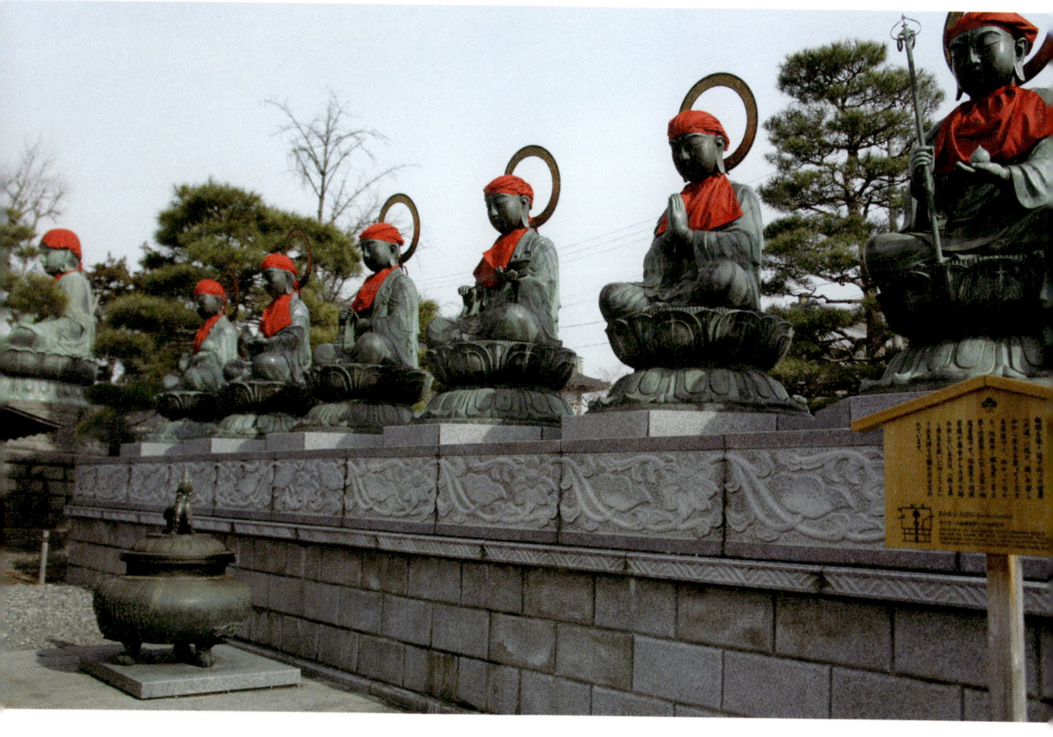

Chapter 2

街の風景

Out & About

Koban　交番

Koban is the common name for the small police boxes that serve as local branch offices of large district police stations. They are manned by between one and a dozen or more policemen (*omawari-san*) on a shift basis. They are generally small two-story structures, some with a striking modern design. There is an office at the front with local maps on the wall and sleeping accommodation above. The versions built on the front of the local policeman's house, mostly in rural areas, are known as *chuzaisho* rather than koban.

　交番とは、大規模な区域警察署の地元の出張所として配置された小規模な派出所の呼び名である。場所によって1人から10数人あまりの警察官（おまわりさん）が配属され、交替で勤務している。ふつうは2階建ての小さな建物だが、中にはモダンなデザインで人目をひく交番もある。正面に近隣の地図を壁にはった執務室があり、2階は宿泊所となっている。地方に見かけることが多いが、地元のおまわりさんの自宅前に建てられた交番は、交番というより駐在所として知られている。

街の風景

Maneki-neko 招き猫

Ornamental *maneki-neko* (beckoning cats) have been popular since the middle of the Edo period as good-luck talismans. Made of clay, porcelain, papier-mâche, wood, or plastic, they are believed to bring good business to shops and restaurants. They are also often displayed as a sign of welcome in the *genkan* entrance of houses. The cats beckon in Japanese-style, with the palm facing outward. Those with the right paw raised are believed to bring good luck in business finance; those with the left paw raised are for welcoming customers or guests.

招き猫は、江戸時代中期から開運のお守りとして人気がある。粘土、磁器、張り子、木、プラスチックなど材質はさまざまだが、商店やレストランに商売繁盛を招くと信じられている。訪問客を歓迎するしるしとして、一般家庭の玄関に置いてあることも多い。猫は、前脚の内側を外へ向けて手招きをする日本式のポーズをとる。右の前脚をあげている招き猫は金運を、左の前脚をあげている招き猫は客を招くとされている。

51

街の風景

Noren のれん

Noren are split curtains made of cloth still hung at the entrance to traditional-style restaurants, shops and public baths. They started off as lengths of cloth that provided shade and kept the street dust from entering the door, like the curtains used in temples. The name of the establishment (*yago*) and maybe the family crest (*mon*) is usually printed on the noren, so in the old days they were the equivalent of the *kanban* signs now seen on the sides of commercial buildings. When the noren is hanging outside, it's a sign that the place is open for business. Noren bearing actors' names traditionally hang at the entrance to theater dressing-rooms.

のれんとは、布製のカーテンを縦に裂いたようなもので、今でも和風の飲食店や商店、銭湯などの入り口に掲げられている。寺で使われていた垂れ幕のように、日除けやほこり除けに用いた1枚の布から始まった。ふつう、店の称号(屋号)や家の紋章(紋)が印刷されており、のれんは、その昔、現在の商業ビルの看板に相当するものだった。外にのれんがかかっているときは営業中のしるし。役者の名前が入ったのれんを劇場の楽屋の入り口にかけるのも伝統の1つだ。

53

街の風景

Nawa-noren 縄のれん

There are several words for casual drinking and eating establishments, including *izakaya* (remain + liquor store; i.e. drinking at a liquor store), *akachochin* (red lanterns), and *nomiya* (drinking place). Another term, less heard these days, is *nawa-noren*, after a special type of noren made of many straw cords hanging over the entrance. The phrase *nawa-noren o kuguru* (go under the straw cords) used to be a common phrase for going for some cheap drink and food.

　気軽に立ち寄れる飲食店には、居酒屋（「居る」+「酒屋」、すなわち酒屋で飲むこと）、赤ちょうちん（赤い提灯）、飲み屋（飲むところ）など、いくつかの呼び名がある。最近はあまり耳にしないが、縄のれんもその呼び名の1つで、たくさんの縄ひもでつくった独特ののれんが店の入り口にかかっていることからその名がついた。「縄のれんをくぐる」という言い回しは、安い店に飲み食いに行くときによく使われていた。

55

街の風景

Chochin   提灯

Chochin are paper lanterns for outside use that can be hung from the eaves or carried. They can still be seen in many colors and sizes all over Japan and serve many different purposes, although today they usually contain an electric light bulb rather than the traditional candle. They are generally made of tough paper attached to collapsible bamboo hoops. Many chochin, especially red ones (*akachochin*), hang outside restaurants and drinking places to advertise the establishment's name or what it serves. White and yellow chochin can often be seen at shrines and temples, and in festivals they may bear patrons' names.

　提灯とは屋外で使用する紙製の手さげランプのことで、軒下にぶら下げたり携行したりすることができる。色やサイズはさまざまで、今でも各地で多種多様な目的に使用されている。しかし、近年は、光源に昔からのろうそくの代わりに電球を使うのが一般的である。通常、折りたためる輪状の竹ひごに丈夫な和紙を貼り付けてつくる。とくに赤色をした提灯（赤ちょうちん）など、店名や食べ物を知らせる目的でレストランや飲み屋の外につるされている提灯は多い。神社や寺でしばしば見かける白や黄色の提灯は、祭りのときは後援者の名前が入ることもある。

街の風景

Shokuhin sanpuru 食品サンプル

Many restaurants have display windows featuring realistic models of many of the dishes and drinks on the menu, plus their prices. This is especially true of the restaurant floor of department stores, where the idea originated. A fine display draws customers, and even if you can't read the menu, you can always go outside and point at a model!

The hand-painted models are called *shokuhin sanpuru* (food sample). This sensible idea was developed in Tokyo in the early 20th century as unusual dishes from overseas began to appear. The models used to be made of wax, but today silicon molds of actual food items are taken and then liquid vinyl models are made.

メニューにある料理や飲み物を、その本物そっくりの模型に値段も添えてショーウインドーに陳列してあるレストランは多い。とりわけあてはまるのがこのアイデアの発祥地とされるデパートのレストラン階だ。素晴らしいディスプレーは客の目を奪い、たとえメニューが読めなくても、ショーウインドーの所に行ってその模型を指さすだけで用が足りる！

この手塗りの模型は食品サンプルと呼ばれる。気の利いたこのアイデアは、海外からなじみの薄い料理が入り始めた20世紀初めの東京で始まった。かつてはろうで作っていたが、現在は実物の食品からシリコンで型をとり、ビニール樹脂でつくっている。

街の風景

Daruma だるま

Legless, armless, neckless *daruma* dolls made of wood, plastic, stone or papier-mâche over a bamboo frame can be seen all over Japan. They often have a rounded, weighted base so that they will always roll back upright when tipped over, symbolizing a spirit of never giving up. The name comes from the Indian Buddhist priest Boddhidharma, regarded as the founder of Zen Buddhism, who traveled to China in the 6th century. He is said to have meditated staring at a wall for nine years until he was unable to use his legs, and he cut off his eyelids so that he would never doze off. The common red color of daruma dolls is based on an Indian priest's dress.

　脚、腕、首のないだるまは、木やプラスチックや石、または竹枠を用いた張り子でつくる人形で、日本各地で目にすることができる。多くは、底が重くて丸い形をしているので倒しても必ず起き上がることから、不屈の精神を表している。名前の由来はインドの禅僧、菩提達磨。禅宗の開祖といわれ、6世紀に中国を旅した人物だ。彼は9年もの間、脚を動かせなくなるまで壁に向かって瞑想を続け、決して居眠りをしないように、まぶたを切り落としたそうだ。広く知られただるまの赤色はインドの僧侶が着ていた服の色である。

61

街の風景

Kokeshi こけし

Kokeshi are a unique type of cylindrical wooden doll with a rounded head and no arms or legs. Kokeshi carving developed as a winter activity of woodcarvers and farmers in the Tohoku region of northern Japan in the 19th century. Traditional dolls have hand-painted faces and floral kimono designs, mostly red with black hair and simple facial features, though some are painted entirely in black. The head is often removable; some Miyagi Prefecture dolls let out a charming squeak when it's revolved. Kokeshi are made from various types of wood with a nice grain, *sakura* cherry wood being popular. They develop a pleasant patina with age and should occasionally be polished with a soft cotton *tenugui* towel. Kokeshi-shaped ornaments include toothpick-holders, pencils, erasers and mobile phone straps.

　こけしは独特な円筒形の木製人形で、球体の頭部があり、腕と脚がない。こけし彫りは、19世紀の北日本の東北地方で、木彫師や農民たちの間で冬の間の活動として広まったものだ。伝統的なこけしは手描きの顔と花柄の着物姿で、着物の多くは赤で描かれ、黒い髪の毛に、素朴な顔立ちをしている。中には黒一色で彩色されたものもある。頭部はしばしばとりはずしができる。宮城県でつくられたこけしには、頭部を回すとキュッキュッと音が鳴る仕掛けのものがある。こけしは木目の美しいさまざまな種類の木でつくられる。中でも桜の木は人気が高い。長い年月を経ると表面に美しいつやが出るこけしは、ときおり、やわらかい木綿の日本手ぬぐいで磨くとよい。こけしをかたどった装飾品も多く、つま楊枝入れや鉛筆、消しゴム、携帯ストラップなどがある。

63

街の風景

Maiko 舞妓

Maiko are young female entertainers, usually in their late teens, who entertain guests at private parties in Kyoto by performing traditional music, dancing and singing, pouring drinks, and playing games. They can easily be recognized by their distinctive appearance: colorful kimonos with seasonal motifs, very long drooping sashes, fancy ornamental hairpins (*kanzashi*), and high platform sandals like clogs. They also use traditional makeup: red and black on a white foundation like a mask. They are actually undergoing rigorous training to become a *geiko*, the name used in Kyoto for geisha. These days, many female visitors to Kyoto, Japanese and foreign, enjoy dressing up as a maiko for the day.

舞妓は一般に10代後半の若い女性で、京都で催される個人的な宴会で伝統的な音楽を演奏したり、踊りや唄を披露したり、酒をついだり、ゲームに興じるなど、宴会客の接待を仕事とする芸人である。季節の柄が入った色鮮やかな着物、だらりの帯、意匠を凝らした髪飾り（かんざし）、そしてぽっくり下駄という特徴のある装いによって、舞妓であることはすぐに見分けがつく。白塗りの下地に赤と黒の色を使った面のような化粧もまた伝統的である。京都では芸者のことを芸妓と呼ぶが、舞妓はその芸妓になるまでの厳格な修行中にある見習い段階の者をいう。最近は、日本人、外国人を問わず、京都を訪れる観光客でにわか舞妓の扮装を楽しむ女性が多い。

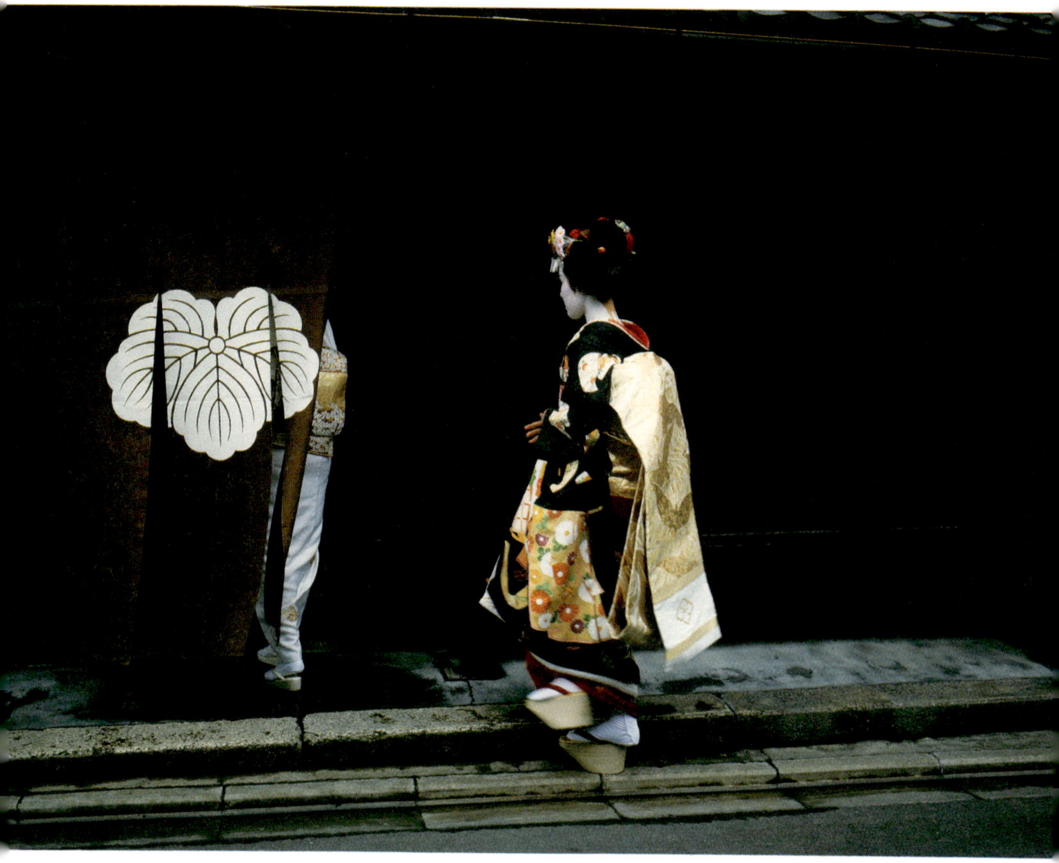

Chapter 3

冠婚葬祭

Ceremonial Occasions & Items

Shinzen-kekkonshiki 神前結婚式

Most Japanese hold a traditional Shinto *shinzen-kekkonshiki* wedding ceremony, attended by a *kannushi* priest, *miko* shrine maidens, and close family members and friends. The couple wear formal wedding kimonos (*kekkon-isho*). The groom (*hanamuko*) wears a kimono with gray split-trousers (*hakama*) and a long, loose black jacket (*haori*) bearing his family crest (*mon*). For the official ceremony the bride (*hanayome*) wears a long overgarment (*uchikake*) over a white wedding kimono (*shiromuku*). White is traditionally the color of death in Japan, so it symbolizes both the death of the bride's natural ties to her parents and a willingness to dye the garment in the color of her husband's family. She may change into a colorful *iro-uchikake* kimono before the reception as a sign she has become a member of her husband's family, and change again during the party into a Western dress, just to be fashionable!

大多数の日本人は伝統的な神道にのっとった神前結婚式を挙げる。神主や巫女、近親者や友人が列席する。新郎新婦は正式な結婚式用の着物（結婚衣装）を身につける。花婿は家の紋章（紋）の入った紋付羽織袴を着る。花嫁は、式の間は白い着物（白無垢）の上に身丈の長い上着（打ち掛け）を羽織る。日本では、昔から白は死を象徴する色とされており、白い衣装は花嫁の実家との生来のつながりを絶つことと、その白い衣装を嫁ぎ先の色に染めるという意志の両方を象徴する。披露宴が始まる前に花嫁はあざやかな色打ち掛けに着替えることがある。これは夫の家の一員となったしるしを表す。そして披露宴の途中で再び西洋風のドレスに着替えることもあるが、これは単におしゃれのためだ！

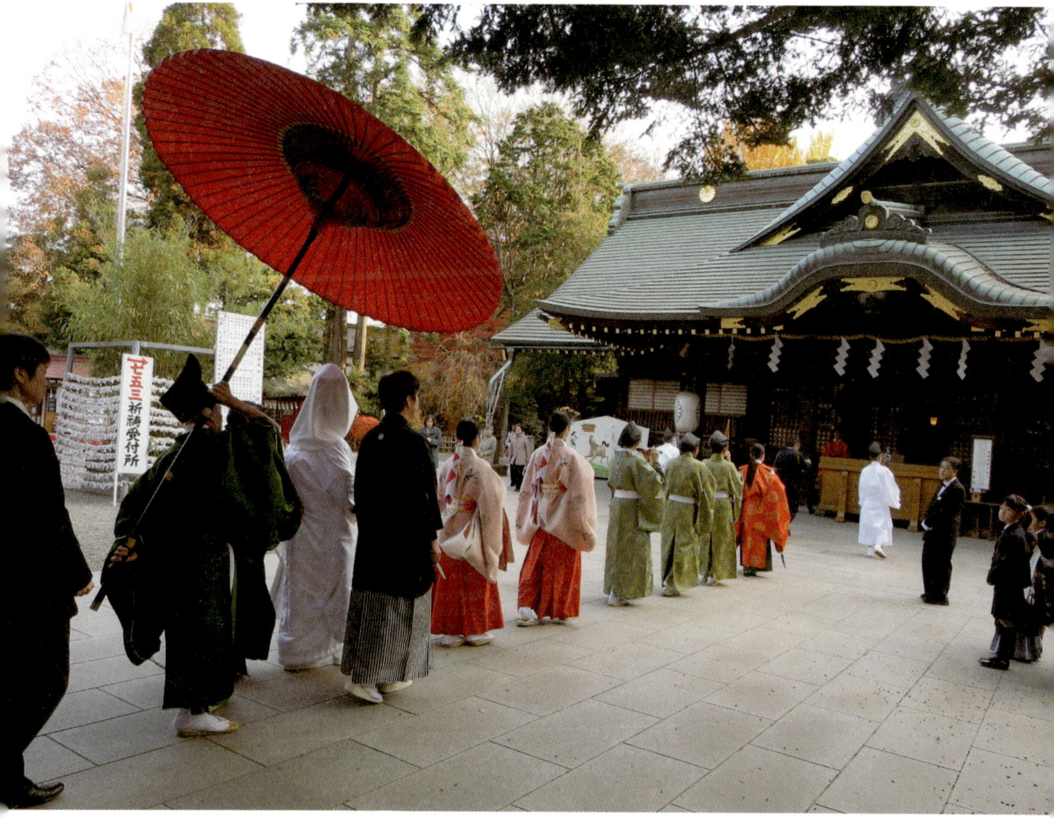
七五三
祈祷受付所

Tsuno-kakushi　角隠し

A bride's hair is arranged in a traditional *bunkin-takashimada* style with various ornamental hairpins. Instead of a Western-style veil, there are two choices of hair covering. One is a large white band called a *tsuno-kakushi* (horn-cover) which is said to hide a woman's 'horns' and indicate her obedience to her husband, although most brides these days probably never think of the symbolism! The tsuno-kakushi is often worn at the start of the reception party as well. The other covering is a kind of large white silk bonnet called a *wataboshi*, designed so that the bride's face is only properly visible to her husband. This is usually removed before the reception.

花嫁の髪は、さまざまな飾りのかんざしを使って伝統的な文金高島田に整えられる。西洋式のベールの代わりに髪を覆うものとして2通りある。1つは角隠しと呼ばれる大きな白い帯状の布で、女性の「角」を隠し夫への従順さを表すものとされるが、おそらく今日の花嫁たちはほとんどがそんな象徴的意味合いなど考えもしないだろう！　角隠しは披露宴の開始時にかぶることも多い。もう1つは綿帽子と呼ばれる大きな白い絹のボンネットのようなもので、花嫁の顔が花婿だけに見えるようになっている。これは披露宴が始まる前にはずすのがふつうだ。

冠婚葬祭

Shio 塩

Salt is regarded as the great element of purification in Japan; it is believed to be effective in providing balance, warding off evil spirits, and generating strength. It features in many Shinto rites. One example is the salt thrown by sumo wrestlers before each bout to purify both themselves and the ring (*dohyo*). Salt is also sprinkled on an empty plot of land at a ground-breaking ceremony (*jichinsai*) to pacify the god of the soil. Another example is *mori-jio*, small conical mounds of salt placed on a saucer at one or both sides of the entrance to a house to purify all those who enter. Similar piles are sometimes seen outside restaurants today.

　日本では、塩はお清めに欠かせない大切な要素である。塩はバランスをもたらし、悪霊を追い払い、力を生み出すと信じられている。神道の儀式には頻繁に登場する。力士が取組前に塩をまくのも、自分自身と土俵を清めるためだ。地鎮祭の鍬(くわ)入れ式でも、土地の神を鎮めるため、更地に塩をまく。そのほかの例として、盛り塩がある。家の入り口の片側あるいは両側に、皿に小さく円すい形に盛った塩を置き、その家に入る人たちを清めるというものである。飲食店の外に同じように盛られた塩を目にすることもある。

73

冠婚葬祭

Juzu 数珠

A *juzu* (counting beads) is a Buddhist rosary that believers hold in their hand for counting while repeating the *Namu-amidabutsu* chant, or wear round their neck. A complete rosary is a ring of 108 beads (*honren-juzu* or *nirin-juzu*), representing the 108 earthly desires which should be avoided. There are shorter versions with 54, 42, 27, 21, or 14 beads and larger ones with up to 1,080 beads. The beads are generally made from sandalwood, nuts, or quartz, and come in different sizes. The tassels on the juzu represent we humans who have those desires. The way the beads are strung together varies depending on the sect. Many people carry a small juzu when they visit a grave or attend a Buddhist funeral (*soshiki*) or memorial service (*hoji*). Kyoto is the main center of juzu production.

数珠（数え珠）は仏教徒にとってのロザリオである。信者は、「南無阿弥陀仏」を繰り返し唱える間、その回数を数えるために数珠を手にかけて持つ、あるいは首にかける。正式の数珠には珠が108ある（本連数珠、または二輪数珠）。これはこの世のはらうべき108つの煩悩を表している。54、42、27、21、あるいは14珠しかない短めの数珠や、数の多いものもあり、最長のものは1,080珠もある。珠はふつう白檀、木の実、水晶などでできており、サイズはさまざまである。数珠の房は、煩悩を持つ私たち人間を表している。珠のつなぎ方は宗派によって異なる。墓参りに行くときや仏式の葬式や法事に出席するときは、小さな数珠を持参する人が多い。数珠の主たる生産地は京都である。

75

冠婚葬祭

Mokugyo 木魚

A *mokugyo* (wooden fish) is a rounded wooden drum used during the chanting of Buddhist sutras, both in temples and at private homes. Struck rhythmically like a gong, it produces a mellow kind of sound. Carved from a single piece of wood, often camphorwood, mokugyo usually sit on a small *zabuton* cushion and are in the shape of a fat fish. With a slit at one end to represent the fish's mouth and often carved with fish scales, mokugyo are related historically to the hanging wooden fish used as dinner gongs at Zen temples. There is a rounded handle at one end, which may be intricately carved; some handles have a design of dragons holding a sacred jewel. The end of the wooden beater is padded with cloth, rubber or leather. Some mokugyo resemble a human skull.

　「木の魚」を意味する木魚は、寺や家庭でお経を上げるときに使う、丸みのある木製の鼓のことである。どらのようにリズミカルにたたくとやわらかい感じの音がする。たいていはクスノキだが1本の木をくりぬいてつくられ、小さな座布団状のクッションの上に置く。木魚はまるまると肥えた魚の形をしている。一方の端に魚の口を表すスリットがあり、うろこを彫りつけてあることが多く、禅寺で食事の合図に使用された魚の形をした木製のどらと歴史的に関係がある。もう一方の端には丸みのある持ち手があり、ここにも手の込んだ彫刻が施されていることがある。たとえば宝珠を持った龍の姿を刻んだ持ち手もある。木魚をたたくバチの先端は布やゴム、皮革などの当て物が施されている。見ようによっては人間の頭がい骨に似ている木魚もある。

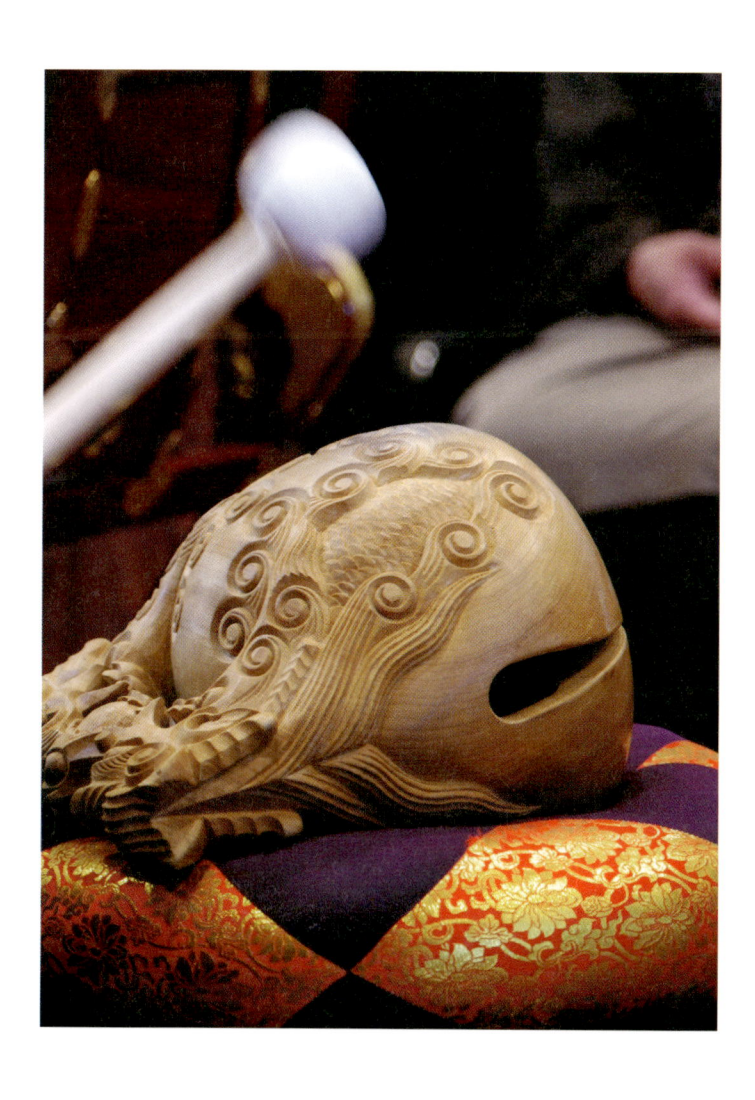

冠婚葬祭

Mizuhiki　水引

Japan has a long tradition of wrapping presents carefully and beautifully. This denotes respect, and also reflects the practice of presents not being opened in the presence of the giver. Formal gifts are covered in a sheet of high quality white paper called *hoshogami* and then tied with *mizuhiki* cords and decorated with a *noshi*. Mizuhiki are stiff cords made from mulberry pulp paper which has been soaked in the water used to rinse rice and then hardened. Sometimes mizuhiki are made into complex designs of lucky creatures such as cranes and turtles to accompany the betrothal gifts exchanged by families before a wedding.

日本には贈り物をていねいに、かつ美しく包む伝統がある。これは相手に対する敬意を表すと同時に、もらった物をその場で開けない習慣を反映している。正式な贈り物は奉書紙と呼ばれる白い高級紙で包み、水引と呼ばれるひもで縛り、のしで飾る。水引は、米のとぎ汁に浸して丈夫にしたクワの木のパルプ紙からできた固いひもである。鶴や亀など、縁起のいい動物を複雑なデザインに結んだ水引は、結納をとり交わすときの贈り物などに使われる。

79

冠婚葬祭

Noshi のし

Noshi (short for *noshiawabi*, stretched abalone) is a lucky decoration added to the special envelope for gifts of money at weddings or funerals (*noshibukuro*) or the white paper wrapper that goes around a gift. Always placed in the upper right corner, it originally consisted of a folded red and white paper envelope holding a strip of dried abalone (*awabi*). These days a strip of yellow paper is generally used instead, or the noshi is printed on the wrapper or envelope (*noshigami*). There is often a message printed on the noshigami, such as *Go-kekkon iwai* (Congratulations on your marriage), but if you want a message-free noshigami wrapper you can ask for *muji-noshi*.

のしは、のしあわびの略で、結婚式や葬式などの祝儀や香典を包む特殊な封筒(のし袋)や贈り物にかぶせるのし紙に添える縁起のよい装飾品である。必ず右上のすみに置くのしは、もともとは干したあわびの細片を薄く伸ばした(のした)もので、折りたたんだ紅白の紙に包まれていた。近ごろは、一般に黄色い紙片を代用したり、あるいは、最初からのしが印刷されたのし紙や封筒もある。「ご結婚祝い」など祝いの言葉が印刷されているのし紙がよくあるが、表書きが不要な場合は「無地のし」を頼めばよい。

冠婚葬祭

Chapter 4

遊 び

Games

Shogi　将棋

The two major board games in Japan are *shogi* and *igo* (often called just *go*). They are both for two players and are extremely popular, particularly with men.

Shogi is very similar to chess, the aim being to checkmate the opponent's king (*osho*). Each player begins with 20 five-sided pointed pieces, all bearing a name written in kanji characters. There are equivalents of rooks, bishops, knights and pawns, but no queens. The two major differences from chess are the ability to use captured pieces and change the strength of pieces when they are inside enemy territory. The board has 81 squares (9×9).

盤を使った日本の２大ゲームは将棋と囲碁（単に「碁」と呼ばれることが多い）だ。どちらも２人で対戦するもので、広く普及している。とくに男性に愛好者が多い。

　将棋はチェスによく似たゲームで、対戦相手の王（王将）を詰めていくのがねらいである。対戦者それぞれが、すべて漢字で名前が書いてある五角形の駒20個を並べて試合を始める。チェスのルーク、ビショップ、ナイト、ポーンに相当する駒があるが、クイーンはない。チェスとの大きな違いは、とった駒を自分のものとして使える点と、敵陣に飛び込むと駒の威力を変えられるという２点だ。盤には縦横９マス、計81のマスがある。

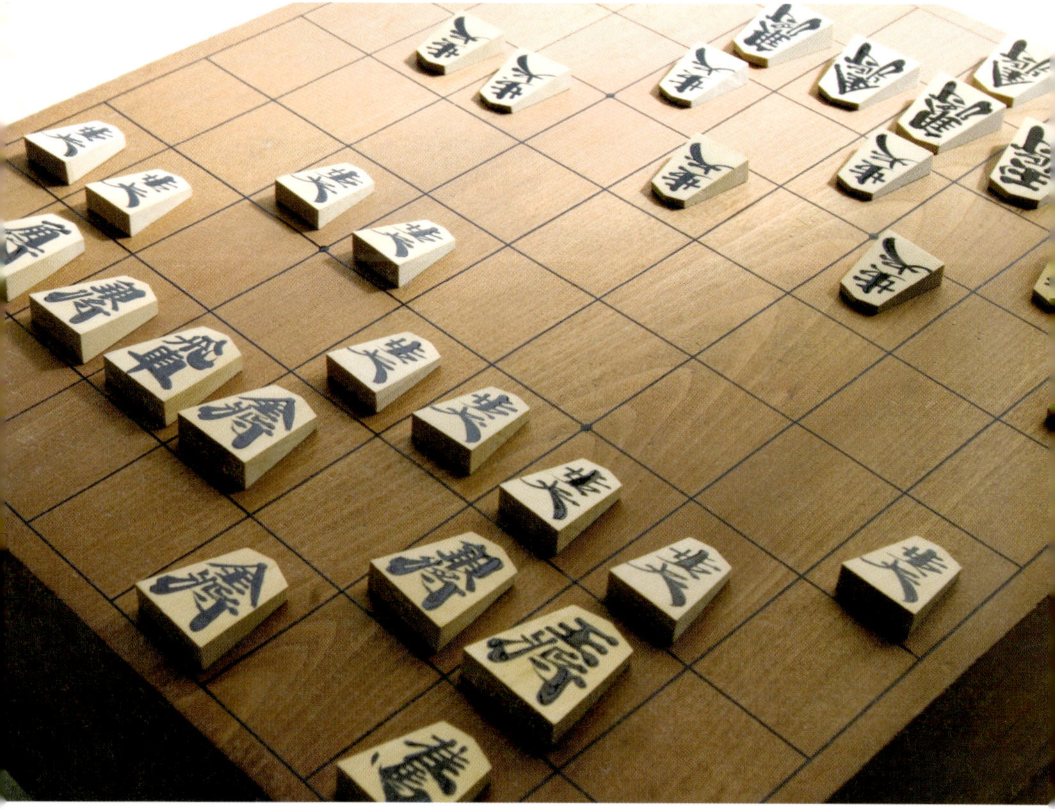

Go 碁

The ancient game of *go* developed from the Chinese game of Wei-chi around the 6th century. Regarded by many as an art, it's played with disk-shaped black and white stones (*ishi*). There are 181 black 'crow' stones made from a kind of slate—for the player who starts the game—and 180 white 'heron' stones traditionally made from shell. They are kept in round wooden pots called *goke*, *goki* or *gotsubo*. The traditional wooden board (*goban*) is marked out with a mesh of black lacquered lines to create 361 (19×19) intersecting points (*me* or *moku*) on which the players place stones in turn. The aim is to gain territory and capture your opponents' stones by surrounding them. There are said to be more possible moves than all the atoms in the universe!

　古来からの遊びである碁は、6世紀ごろに中国のWei-chiというゲームから発達した。碁はアートだとみなす人が多く、ゲームは円盤状の黒と白の石を使って行われる。ある種のスレートからつくられる黒の石「カラス」は181個あり、先手をとるプレイヤーが使う。白い石「鷺」は180個ある。昔から、白い石は貝殻からつくられる。石は碁笥、碁器あるいは碁壺と呼ばれる木製の丸い容器に入れておく。伝統的な木製の碁盤は、盤上に黒い漆で網の目のように線が引かれており、19×19の361目(「め」または「もく」)の交点がある。対局者はこの目に交互に石を置いていく。自分の陣地を確保し、相手の石を囲んで獲得していくのがねらいである。可能な打ち方は宇宙に存在するすべての原子の数よりも多い、と言われている。

遊び

Hanetsuki 羽根つき

At one time, a common sound on the streets on New Year's Day was the 'kon-kon' of shuttlecocks (*hane*) being hit by wooden battledores (*hagoita*) in a game resembling badminton. However, no net is used; the idea is simply to keep the shuttlecock in the air. Mostly played by girls dressed in kimono, it's called *hanetsuki*. Today, however, you rarely hear the sound because most children are more interested in modern pursuits such as video games, and it's also become more dangerous to play out on the streets. Hagoita remain popular in the form of lucky ornaments for display (*kazari-hagoita*), especially at the New Year, with topical designs featuring famous sportspeople, politicians, actors, TV stars, and manga and anime characters.

　かつて元旦の往来でよく耳にした音は、木製の羽子板で羽根をたたく「コーンコーン」という音だった。その遊びはバドミントンに似ていた。もっともネットは使わず、単に羽根が宙に浮いた状態をどれだけ長く維持できるかという発想である。たいていは着物を着た女の子たちが遊んでいたもので、羽根つきと呼ばれる。しかし今ではその音を聞くことはめったにない。というのも、ほとんどの子供たちはテレビゲームなどの最新の遊びに興味が向いているし、また往来で遊ぶことが危険になったからでもある。羽子板は幸運を呼ぶ装飾品（飾り羽子板）として今でも高い人気を維持している。とりわけお正月になると、人気のスポーツ選手、政治家、俳優、タレント、漫画やアニメのキャラクターなどを取り上げた話題性のあるデザインが見られる。

遊び

Koma コマ

Tops (*koma*) have been spinning in Japan for well over 1,000 years. Wooden tops unearthed from 8th century ruins show that they had entered Japan from China and Korea by the Nara period. Made of wood, bamboo, metal or plastic, they come in many shapes and sizes; some have a protruding rod for spinning with the fingers, others use strings, and some even make pleasant humming sounds. Top-spinning became a feature of New Year festivities around the end of the 19th century.

　日本には千年をはるかに超える昔から、コマを回す風景があった。8世紀の遺跡から木製のコマが発掘されたことから、コマは奈良時代までに中国や朝鮮から日本に入ってきたことがわかる。木製のものもあれば竹製、金属製、プラスチック製など種類も豊富で、コマの形やサイズはさまざまだ。上に棒が突き出ている形のものは指で回すが、ほかの形のものはひもを使って回す。回すとブンブンと心地よい音が出るコマもある。コマ回しがお正月の行事になったのは19世紀末ごろだ。

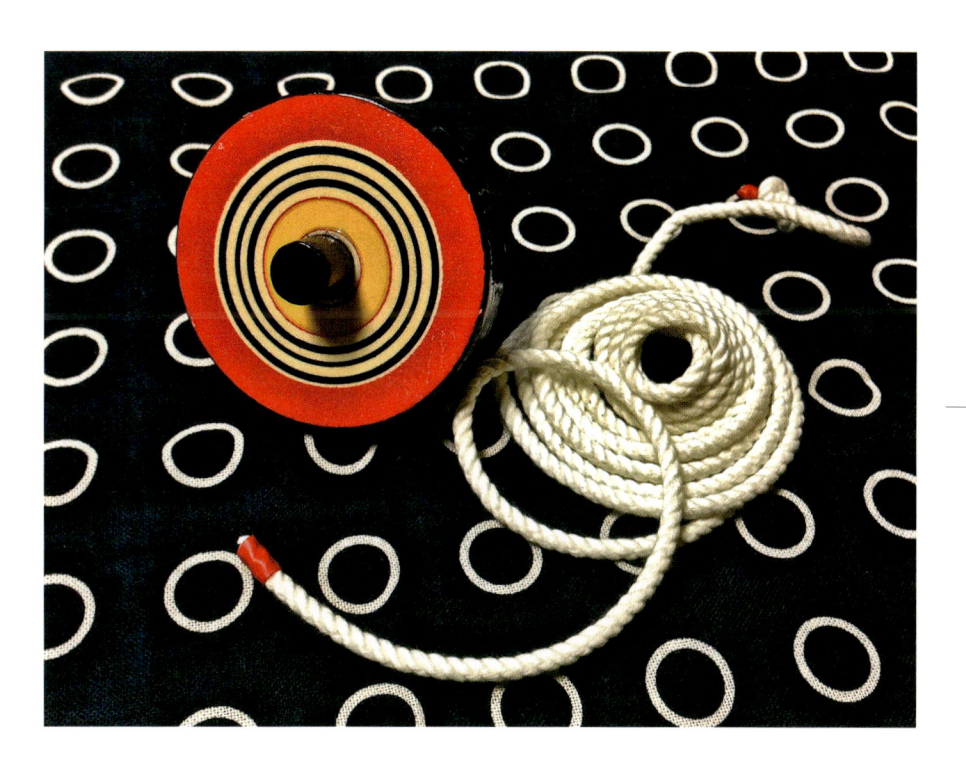

遊び

Tako　たこ

The Japanese word for a kite is *tako*. Kite-flying (*tako-age*) used to be a popular outdoor activity at the New Year, although it is not seen so much today. However, many people still enjoy flying kites all year round, and major kite competitions are held in various locations. Kites have long been treasured for their artistic value, and they make stunning souvenirs.

　　Kites have a long history in Japan and they have been used in various ways. Originally they had the religious meaning of linking heaven and earth. Later, they were used by military commanders for sending messages, and by samurai to announce the birth of a baby boy. During the Edo period, many different designs and shapes evolved: dragons, lions, warriors, woodblock print images (*nishiki-e-dako*), figures, masks, calligraphy, birds and insects.

　　kiteを意味する日本語はたこである。たこあげもお正月に人気の屋外の遊びであったが、現代ではあまり見られなくなった。しかし今でも1年を通して楽しむ人は多く、各地でたこあげの大きな競技会が開かれている。たこは昔から、その芸術的価値が高く評価されており、非常に魅力的なお土産になる。
　　日本におけるたこの歴史は古く、いろいろな用途で使われてきた。もともとたこには天と地をつなぐという宗教的な意味があった。のちに、戦で武将が伝令を出したり、侍が男の子の誕生を知らせるために使われるようになった。江戸時代には数多くのデザインや形が生まれた。龍、獅子、武士、浮世絵（錦絵だこ）、だるま、仮面、筆文字、鳥、昆虫などである。

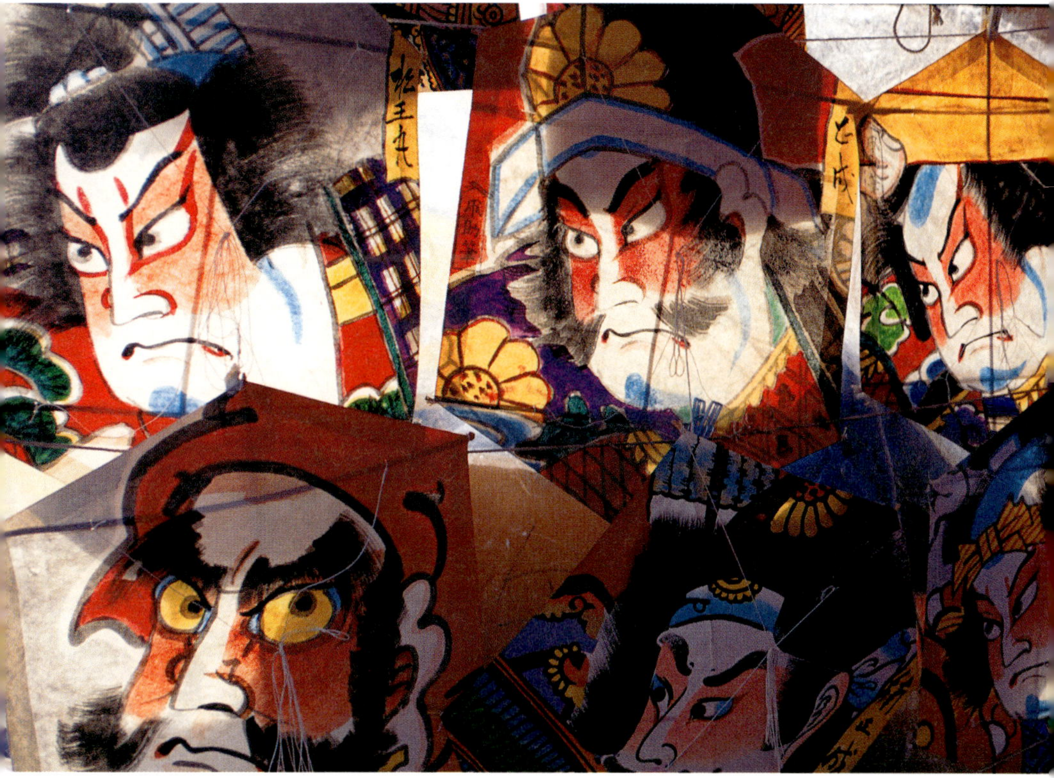
松王丸

Sugoroku すごろく

Sugoroku (double six) is a dice and board game that has gone through many changes over the centuries and has been compared to backgammon, pachisi, ludo, Monopoly and snakes-and-ladders! There are ancient board versions (*ban-sugoroku*) as well as many types using a picture trail (*e-sugoroku*). In the Shoso-in Treasure House of Todaiji Temple in Nara, you can see a board used by the 45th emperor, Shomu in the 8th century. It's a game that today is often given away with children's magazines, featuring topical personalities and cartoon characters.

　すごろく（ダブルシックス）は、さいころとボードを使ったゲームで、何世紀もの間に多くの変化を遂げた。バックギャモンやインドすごろく、ルードー、モノポリー、スネークス・アンド・ラダーズなどと似ているといわれる！古来の盤を使った盤すごろくや数多くの絵のコースを使った絵すごろくがある。奈良の東大寺にある正倉院の宝庫では、8世紀に在位した第45代聖武天皇が使った盤を見ることができる。近ごろは、話題の有名人や漫画のキャラクターを描いたすごろくが、子供向けの雑誌のふろくになることが多い。

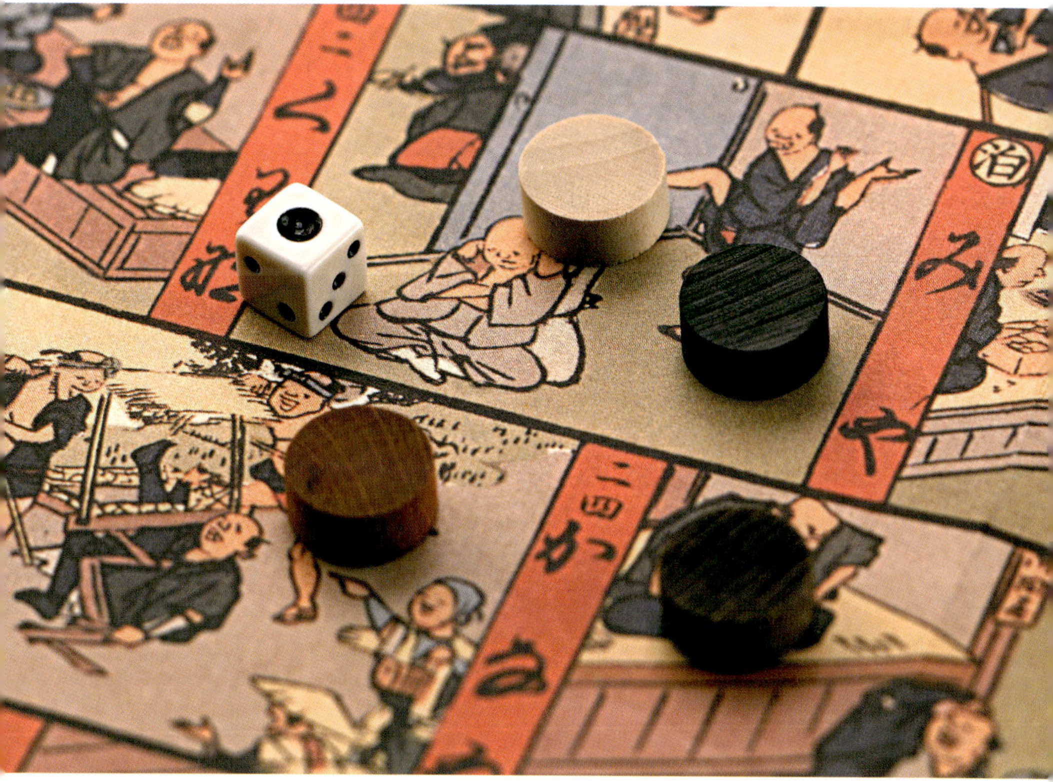
泊

Karuta かるた

The term *karuta* (from the Portuguese word *carta*) refers to several types of cards featuring pictures, numbers or calligraphy that are used for playing various card games, especially at the New Year. Today there are many sets to help children learn Japanese and foreign languages, including English.

Playing cards (now called *toranpu*) were introduced to Japan by Portuguese sailors visiting Nagasaki in the 16th century. Long before that, however, Japanese nobles were playing games in which the two halves of clamshells had to be matched (*kai-awase*).

かるたという言葉(ポルトガル語のcartaに由来する)は、絵や数字、筆文字が描かれた数種類のカードを指し、とくに新年に行われるさまざまなカードゲームに使用される。今日、子どもたちの日本語や英語などの外国語学習に役立つかるたがたくさん出回っている。

カードゲーム(今では「トランプ」と呼ばれている)は、16世紀に長崎を訪れたポルトガル人の船員によって日本にもたらされた。しかし、それよりずっと前に、日本の貴族は2つに割った二枚貝の対を見つける遊びをしていた(貝合わせ)。

97

遊び

Hanafuda 花札

A card game often played at the New Year is *hanafuda*, also known as *hana-karuta* (flower cards). It developed from Dutch card games introduced in the 16th century and ancient Japanese flower picture matching games. The deck consists of 48 different cards divided into 12 suits, each representing a different month. They are illustrated with bold, stylized pictures—mostly in red, blue and black—of flowers, birds and animals appropriate to each season. The cards are smaller and thicker than playing cards. There are many different rules associated with collecting suits.

正月によく遊ぶカードゲームに花かるたとしても知られる花札がある。花札は16世紀に入ってきたオランダのカードゲームや古代の日本の花絵合わせから発展したものである。ひと組が48枚のカードで、12組に分けられるが、この12組がそれぞれ異なる月を表している。札には、通常は赤と青と黒の3色で、それぞれの季節に合った花や鳥、動物が、力強い様式化された絵で描かれている。札はトランプよりも小さくて厚みがある。そろえる組札についてのルールは多岐にわたる。

遊び

Uta-garuta 歌がるた

In the 13th century, the poet Fujiwara no Teika created a famous anthology of 100 great 31-syllable *waka* poems titled *Ogura Hyakunin-isshu* (100 Poems of 100 Poets). In the Edo period, a matching game using the poems called *uta-garuta* (poem cards) was developed. It eventually developed into a popular New Year parlor game, still played by many families today. There are two sets of pasteboard cards, 100 *yomi-fuda* (reading cards) containing the whole poem and 100 *tori-fuda* (grabbing cards) bearing only the final 14 syllables of the poem. As each poem is read aloud, the contestants have to grab the correct *tori-fuda* from those laid out on the floor. The surprisingly dynamic game is especially popular with women. There is an official association and *Kyogi-karuta* (Competitive Karuta) contests are shown every January on TV.

　13世紀、歌人の藤原定家が31音節からなるすばらしい和歌を100首集めて有名な「百人一首」という名の歌集をつくった。江戸時代にはこの百人一首の上の句と下の句を合わせる歌がるたと呼ばれる遊びが広がった。この遊びはやがてお正月の居間で行うゲームになり、今日でも多くの家庭で楽しまれている。百人一首は、厚紙でつくられた札を2セット使う。すべての和歌が書かれた100枚の読み札と、それぞれの歌の最後の14音節だけが書かれている100枚の取り札である。競技者は、歌が高々と読み上げられると、床に並べられた札からできるだけ速くその歌にマッチする取り札をつかみ取らなければならない。この驚くほどにダイナミックなゲームはとりわけ女性の間で人気がある。公式な協会があり、毎年1月にはテレビで競技かるたという大会のもようが放映される。

101

遊び

Chapter 5

伝統芸能・美術

Features of Traditional Life

Men 面

Masks (*men*) feature a great deal in Japanese culture—in stage plays, festivals, rituals, folk dances and children's role playing. They are made of wood, metal, papier-mâché and plastic. Humorous masks used in *kagura* Shinto dances include *otafuku*, the fat-cheeked goddess of mirth, and *hyottoko*, a silly man's face with pouting lips. There are also masks of various species of demons, such as *tengu* (long-nosed goblins) and the oni (ogres) who appear in the *Setsubun* bean-throwing festival on February 3rd. Masks of manga and anime characters are very popular with children.

　舞台演劇、祭り、儀式、民族舞踊、そして子供のごっこ遊びといった日本文化の中で主要な役割を持つ面は、木や金属、張り子、プラスチックなどでつくられる。神道の舞踊である神楽で使用されるユーモラスな面には、ふくらんだほおをした陽気の女神おたふくと、唇をすぼめてとがらせたこっけいな男ひょっとこがある。また、天狗（鼻の長い鬼）や２月３日の節分祭りの豆まきに登場する鬼など、さまざまな種類の鬼の面がある。マンガやアニメのキャラクターの面は子供たちに大人気だ。

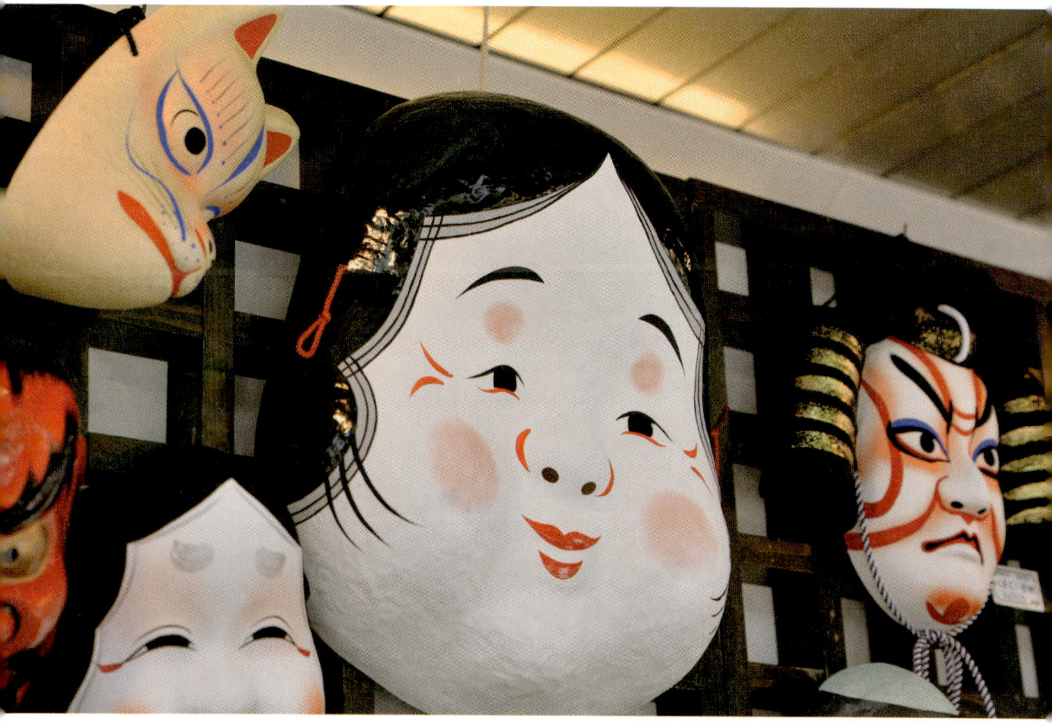

Noh　能

Masks are a very important part of Noh, the ancient performing art that includes music, chanting, stylistic dancing and actors portraying historical figures, priests, demons and ghosts. The main performer, the *shite*, often wears a wooden mask while performing. Each mask is slightly different and Noh actors can express a huge variety of emotions through their subtle head movements. Amongst the most common types of Noh masks are *ko-omote*, a young woman's mask, and *hannya*, representing a female demon with horns. The eye-holes in the masks are very small, so the actors must move around the stage very carefully, using the wooden pillars as positioning guides.

能では面が非常に重要な役割を果たす。能は囃子と謡、舞からなる伝統芸能である。役者たちが演じるのは歴史上の人物や僧侶、鬼、幽霊などだ。シテと呼ばれる主役は、舞台では木製の面をつけることが多い。どの面にも微妙な違いがあり、能の演者はかすかな頭の動きで非常に多彩な感情を演じ分けることができる。最も一般的な能面には、若い女性の面である小面と、角のはえた女の鬼を表す般若がある。面ののぞき穴は非常に小さく視界が限られるので、演者は柱の位置を確認しながら十分に注意して舞台上を動かなければならない。

伝統芸能・美術

Kyogen 狂言

Masks also feature in around 50 of the classical repertoire of 260 short Kyogen comic plays that were historically performed between the very serious Noh dramas, but are often presented independently today. Masks are used for animals, including foxes and *tanuki*, and supernatural beings such as gods and devils. The sons of famous Kyogen actors generally make their demanding stage debut at a very young age dressed in a monkey costume and wearing a mask.

　狂言の古典的レパートリー260作品の内およそ50作品の中にも面が登場する。狂言は、内容が非常にシリアスな芸能である能の合間に伝統的に演じられた短い喜劇であるが、近年は独立して演じられることが多い。キツネやタヌキなどの動物や神や鬼などの超自然的存在を演じるときに面を使う。名高い狂言役者の息子たちはたいてい幼少期に、猿の衣装に猿の面をかぶり過酷な初舞台を踏む。

伝統芸能・美術

Bunraku 文楽

Dating back 400 years, Bunraku theater is a unique combination of *joruri*—stories narrated with musical accompaniment—and puppets who act out the stories in silence. The main characters are operated by three puppeteers. The carved wooden head (*kashira*), operated by the chief puppeteer (*omozukai*), is the most important and expressive part of each puppet. Some of them have movable mouths, eyes and eyebrows. There are around 70 types of kashira, including minor characters with faces resembling traditional Japanese masks.

　400年の歴史を持つ文楽は、音楽を伴って語る物語の浄瑠璃と物語を言葉を発することなく演じる人形で構成されるユニークな演芸である。主役級の登場人物は三人の人形遣いで操る。彫刻を施した木製の頭部（かしら）は、主遣いと呼ばれるシンとなる人形遣いによって操作され、各人形の表情が現われる最も重要な部分だ。中には、口や目や眉が動くかしらもある。かしらは、伝統的な日本の面に似た顔をした端役の登場人物を含め、およそ70種ある。

111

伝統芸能・美術

Ukiyo-e 浮世絵

The Ukiyo-e (pictures of the floating world) genre of art included both paintings and woodblock prints, which are now highly prized by art collectors worldwide. Portraying famous actors, sumo wrestlers, courtesans, legends, and scenes from daily life and famous places, the prints were the equivalent of today's picture postcards, posters and pin-ups, as well as book illustrations. There were also many erotic prints (*shunga*), both for entertainment and instruction. The golden age of Ukiyo-e print production lasted from the 17th century to the late 19th century. The most famous artists are Hiroshige (*53 Stages of the Tokaido*), Hokusai (*36 Views of Mt. Fuji*), Sharaku (Kabuki actors), and Utamaro (beauties).

浮世絵には、肉筆の浮世絵と木版画の浮世絵版画がある。今やどちらも世界中の美術品コレクターの熱い視線を集めている。有名な役者、力士、遊女、伝説的な人物や、日常の風景、そして名所などを描いた浮世絵版画は今日の絵葉書、ポスター、ブロマイドや本の挿絵に相当するものであった。また娯楽と教育を兼ねたエロティックな版画（春画）も多かった。浮世絵制作の全盛期は17世紀から19世紀後半まで続いた。「東海道五十三次」の広重や「富嶽三十六景」の北斎、役者絵の写楽、美人画の歌麿などが最も有名だ。

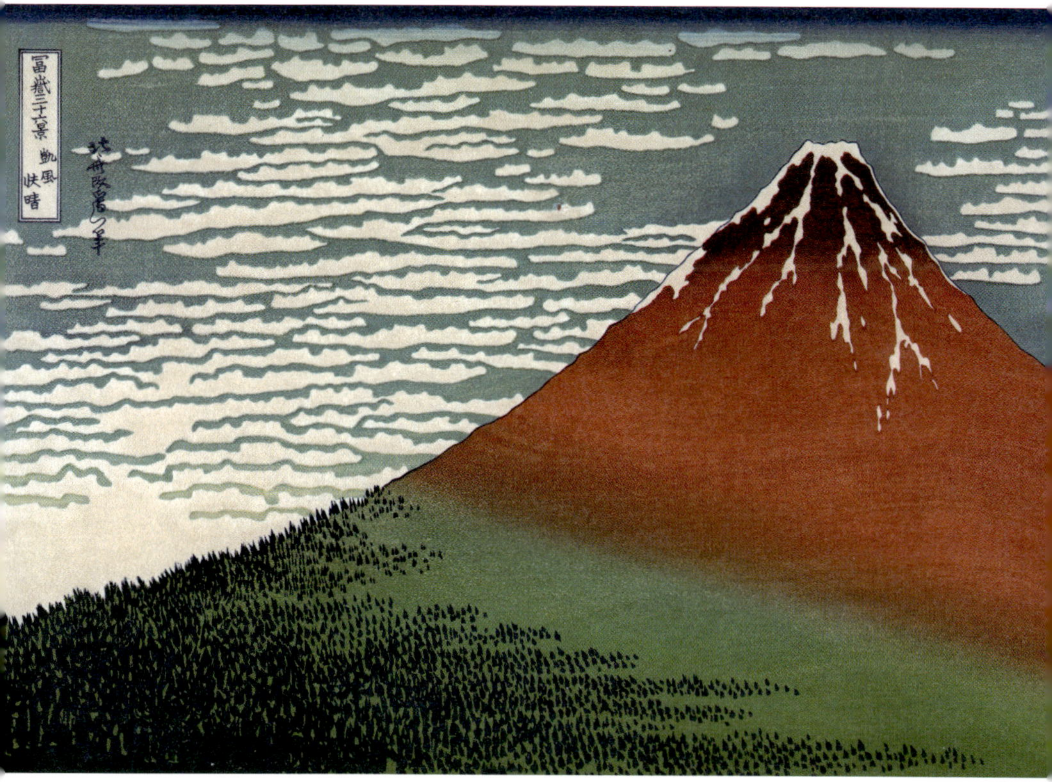
冨嶽三十六景 凱風快晴
北斎改為一筆

There are still craftsmen—Japanese and foreign—producing prints in the traditional way, many of them working alone. However, the production of a woodblock print is a long and difficult process, and it used to be a team effort by specialists: the artist (*ukiyo-e-shi*) who produced the original India ink design; the carvers (*hori-shi*) who carved the blocks, usually of cherry wood; the printers (*suri-shi*) who carefully printed each color, ensuring the paper remained perfectly aligned; and the publisher who dealt with distribution.

今でも伝統的な手法で制作する職人が国籍を問わず存在し、多くは1人で作業している。しかし、木版画の制作は時間と手間がかかるため、かつては何人かの専門家がチームになって制作していた。浮世絵師がオリジナルの絵柄を墨で描き、彫師がふつうは桜材の木版を彫った。刷師は紙が決してずれないように細心の注意をはらいながら1色ごとに刷り、そして出版社が発行を担当した。

115

伝統芸能・美術

Niwa 庭

The long tradition of small, self-contained Japanese gardens (*niwa*) suggesting a whole landscape is alive and well today as a way of making the best use of limited space. They are more for admiring than playing in. Some elements of the gardens around tea ceremony teahouses may be included, such as *tobi-ishi* stepping-stones across gravel or sand, a *sodegaki* ornamental fence adjoining the house, and an *ishidoro* stone lantern. The dry sand, gravel and rock gardens seen at temples are called *karesansui*.

　小さいが、必要なものを完備した一風景を表現する日本庭園（庭）は、限られた空間を最大限に活用する手段として、その長い伝統が今日もしっかりと生きている。日本の庭は、そこで遊ぶというより鑑賞するものだ。茶室の庭には、砂利や砂の上に敷かれた飛び石や、袖垣（建物に取りつける装飾用のフェンス）などが設けられていることもある。寺に見かける乾いた砂、砂利、岩石で構成された庭は枯山水と呼ぶ。

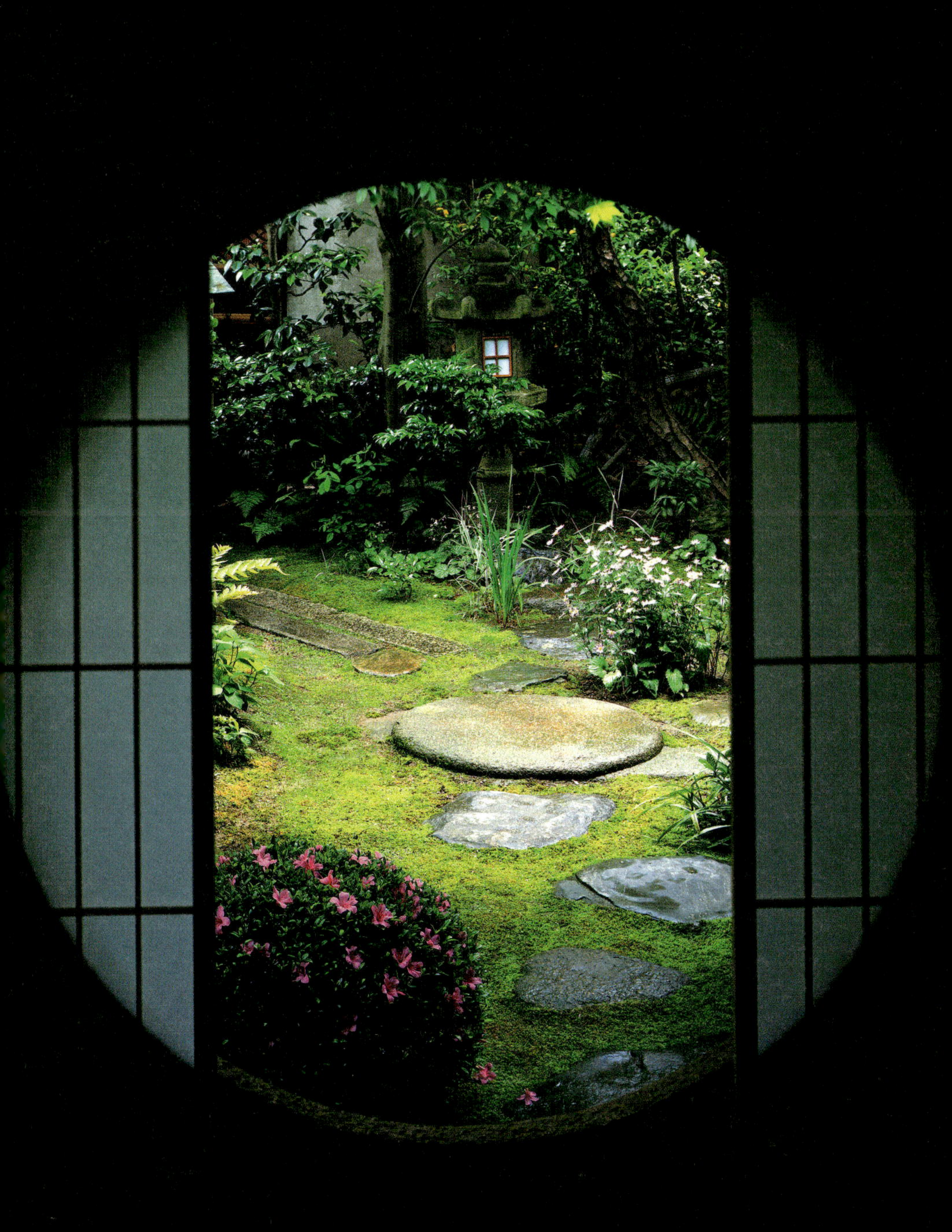

Bonsai 盆栽

The painstaking ancient art of *bonsai* (tray-planting) involves the cultivation of miniature potted trees based on the spirit of *shinzen-bi* (truth, goodness, beauty). It's an interesting combination of manipulating nature while encouraging an appreciation of nature itself. Bonsai can be seen outside people's houses, in *tokonoma* alcoves and at exhibitions. The idea is to create dwarf versions of trees—particularly *matsu* (pine), *keyaki* (zelkova), *sugi* (cedar), *momiji* (maple), *sakura* (cherry) and *hinoki* (cypress)—while maintaining proper proportions with the container, a pleasing asymmetry, and a totally 'natural' look. Bonsai can live for hundreds of years, and their image of immortality makes them popular with the elderly.

　丹精を込めた日本古来の芸術、盆栽とは、真・善・美の精神に基づいたミニチュア鉢植え栽培のこと。自然そのものへの敬意を促す一方で自然を操る、興味深い融合の世界だ。人々は、盆栽を庭に並べたり、床の間に飾ったり、展示会に出品したりする。とりわけ松、けやき、杉、紅葉、桜、ひのきなどの木々の小型版をつくり上げるという発想のもと、鉢との釣り合いや美しく見えるバランスを調整し、完全に「自然な」趣をかもし出す。盆栽は何百年も生き続ける。この不朽のイメージが、年配者層を魅了するのだ。

伝統芸能・美術

Kakejiku 掛け軸

A *kakejiku* hanging picture scroll may include a vertical ink-brush landscape painting (*sansui-ga*), a picture of seasonal birds or flowers (*kacho-ga*), Buddhist images (*butsu-ga*), or a fine piece of calligraphy. Only one kakejiku is displayed in the *tokonoma* alcove of a traditional Japanese room at any one time, usually chosen for its seasonal relevance. The picture in the center is called the *honshi*, and the decorative mounting is the *hyogu*. The scrolls are rolled up and stored in special boxes when not on display.

　掛け軸には、縦長の墨で描いた風景画（山水画）、季節の鳥や花の絵（花鳥画）、仏教関連の絵（仏画）、そして見事な書を表したものなどがある。伝統的な和室の床の間には、ふつう季節感のあるものを選び、一度に一幅だけ飾る。中心となる絵や書を「本紙」、装飾的な枠を「表具」と呼ぶ。ふだんは巻き上げて、専用の箱にしまっておく。

伝統芸能・美術

Ikebana　生け花

An *ikebana* (flowers kept alive) arrangement of flowers, grasses, leaves and berries, carefully chosen to reflect the season, is placed on the matted floor (*toko*) of a tokonoma alcove. In some cases a simple arrangement may be created in a hanging bamboo vase. An incense burner, a valuable ornament, such as a precious stone or carving, or a bonsai may also be on display.

　季節感が重視される花や草や葉や実をアレンジする生け花は、床の間の畳敷きの床に飾る。竹製の花瓶に簡素な生け花を生けることもある。香炉、高価な石や彫刻などの貴重な装飾品、あるいは盆栽なども飾られる。

123

伝統芸能・美術

Shiro 城

Japan's distinctive castles (*shiro*) were developed to deal with the military situation around the end of the 16th and early 17th centuries. Their names consist of the location plus the suffix *-jo*. The main difference from European castles is that only the base ramparts were built of stone. The buildings were all wooden, covered with thick clay and plaster as a defense against fire and attack. However, only a few original structures have survived fires, earthquakes and war damage, so many famous castles, such as Osaka-jo and Nagoya-jo, are actually 20th century reconstructions. The most popular of the dozen or so complete original castle structures that remain today is the beautiful Himeji-jo in Hyogo Prefecture (The White Heron Castle), completed in 1610. It was designated as a World Heritage Site in 1993.

　日本独特の城は、16世紀末から17世紀初めに起こった軍事情勢とともに発達した。城の名称は、所在地の末尾に「城（じょう）」をつける。ヨーロッパの城との大きな違いは、城壁だけが石で築かれているということ。建物はすべて木造で、火災や攻撃から守るために粘土やしっくいを厚く塗ってある。しかし、火事や地震、戦禍を免れて、当時のまま現存する城はごくわずか。大阪城や名古屋城など、有名な城の多くは20世紀になって再建されたものだ。ほぼ完全に当時の姿を残す10数基あまりの城で最も人気があるのは、兵庫県に建つ美しい姫路城（白鷺城）である。1610年に完成した姫路城は1993年に世界文化遺産に登録されている。

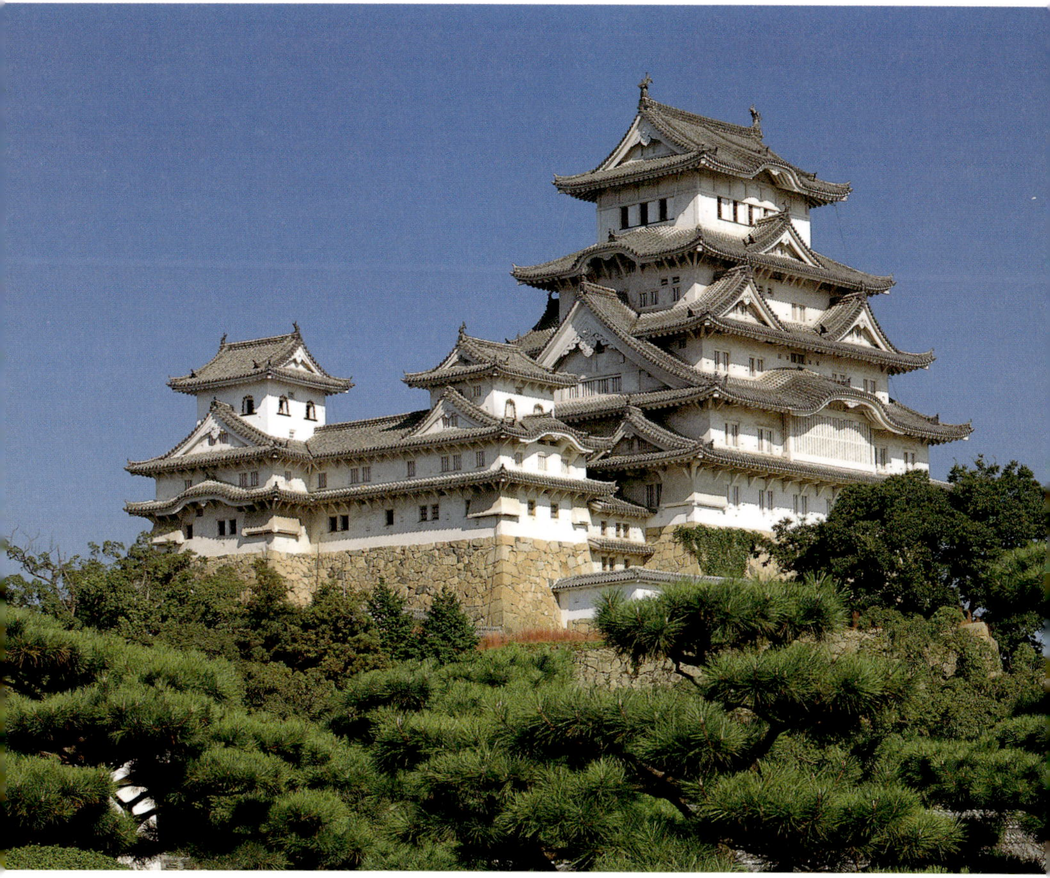

Tenshukaku 天守閣

The high *tenshukaku* keep, or donjon, served as both a watchtower and the last refuge for the lord and his family when a castle was under siege. It was provided with a water supply from a well (*ido*). The two bronze *shachihoko*, mythical creatures like dolphins with lifted tails on the roof of some donjons were believed to protect the castle against fire.

In most cases, an extensive castle town (*jokamachi*) was built around the castle, including temples, entertainment districts and the residences of lower officials. Direct access to the castle was difficult, as castles had at least one wide moat with steep sides (*hori*). In Tokyo, stretches of the inner moat (*uchibori*) and the outer moat (*sotobori*) of Edo Castle can still be seen today, although only a few of the castle's gates (*mon*) remain. The main gate (*otemon*) of castles often consisted of two gates at right angles with a square courtyard between them (*masugata*), in which attackers could be ambushed.

高くそびえたつ天守閣は監視塔であると同時に、城が包囲されたときには、領主とその家族が最後に避難する場所でもあった。水は井戸から供給された。屋根の両端に青銅の鯱が載っている天守閣もある。イルカによく似た想像上の生き物で尾ひれを高く反り上げている鯱は、城を火災から守ると信じられていた。

たいていの場合、城のまわりには城下町が広がり、そこには寺社、歓楽街、下級武士の住居などがあった。どの城も、両側が急勾配になった幅が広い掘が少

なくとも1つはあったため、城内への立入りは容易ではなかった。東京では今でも江戸城の内堀や外堀の広がりを目にすることができるが、現存する門はごくわずかである。城の正門である大手門は、ふつう直角に交わる2つの城門からなることが多く、城門と城門の間は四角い中庭（枡形）になっていて、敵を待ち伏せしやすくなっていた。

Chapter 6

歳時記

Seasonal Features

SPRING

Momo-no-sekku 桃の節句

The *Momo-no-sekku* (Peach Blossom Festival) celebrated on March 3rd centers around girls. It's also called *Joshi-no-sekku* (Festival of the Day of the Snake in early March) or *Hina-matsuri* (The Doll Festival).

The tradition is to set up a display of ceremonial dolls (*hina-ningyo*) wearing court costumes from the Heian period (794–1192). The idea is to pray for the happiness and health of daughters, as well as encourage good behavior and respect for family and ancestors. Dressed up in their finest kimono, girls admire the display dolls, but don't play with them.

桃の節句は、3月3日に祝う女の子の祭り。上巳の節句、あるいはひな祭りともいう。

平安時代 (794 〜 1192) の宮廷衣装をまとう儀式用の人形 (ひな人形) を飾るのが伝統だ。娘たちの幸せと健康を祈り、礼儀と家族や祖先を敬う心を身につけてほしいという願いを込める。女の子たちは一番上等な着物に身を包み、人形飾りを眺めて楽しむが、手にして遊んだりはしない。

歳時記・春

Hina-ningyo　ひな人形

The Hina-ningyo dolls are displayed on a special stand (*hina-dan*), with five or more tiers covered in red cloth or felt. The basic set consists of 15 dolls, depicting an ancient Imperial peach-blossom-viewing party. The top tier features the *o-dairi-sama*, representing the Emperor and Empress in ancient brocade court costumes sitting in front of a gold folded screen. On each side is a *bonbori* floor lamp. On the next tier are three ladies-in-waiting ready to serve sake (*sannin-kanjo*). Below them are five musicians (*gonin-bayashi*), two ministers (*daijin*) with bows and arrows, and finally three footmen (*jicho*), who are sometimes shown as crying, laughing and angry drunks!

ひな人形は、赤い布もしくはフェルトで覆われた5段かそれより多い階段状の特別な台（ひな壇）に飾られる。人形の数は15体が基本で、昔の皇室で行われた桃の花見の宴を表現している。最上段には天皇と皇后を象徴するお内裏さまがいて、金襴の装束を身にまとい、金びょうぶを背にして座る。その両脇にはぼんぼり（床用ランプ）を置く。2段目には、酒をつぐために控えている3体の三人官女。その下の3段目に楽人である5体の五人ばやし、弓と矢を持った2体の大臣、最下段に3体の仕丁と続く。仕丁は、泣きじょうご、笑いじょうご、怒りじょうごを表すことがある！

歳時記・春

Hanami　花見

Since ancient times, the word *hana* (flower) has been synonymous with *sakura* (cherry blossom), which has become the iconic flower of Japan. It's a potent motif for the arrival of spring, blooming around April in central Japan when so many things start, including the school year. It's also regarded as a symbol of worldly transience, blooming briefly and falling quickly. *Hanami* (cherry-blossom viewing) took off as an entertainment with ordinary townspeople around 400 years ago. They started gathering under the cherry trees to eat, drink and be merry. Since the 19th century, the *Somei-yoshino* flowering cherry has been planted nationwide. Being a clone, all the trees bloom at the same time in each location. As the "cherry front" gradually moves from south to north, plastic sheets and cardboard are spread on the ground and hanami party-time begins!

古代から桜は「花」の代名詞とされて、日本を象徴する花になった。春の訪れを表わす強力な存在であり、学校の新学期などさまざまなことが新たに始まる4月ごろに日本の中心部で開花する。咲いたと思えばすぐに散る、そんな桜は浮き世のはかなさを象徴するものでもある。花見の風習はおよそ400年前に一般庶民の娯楽として広まった。桜の木の下に集い、食べたり、飲んだりして楽しんだのである。19世紀以降、ソメイヨシノという品種の桜が全国的に植樹されている。クローン種であるため、それぞれの地域で一斉に開花する。桜前線は南から北へだんだんと移動し、地面にビニールシートや段ボールを敷いた花見の宴会が各地で行われる。

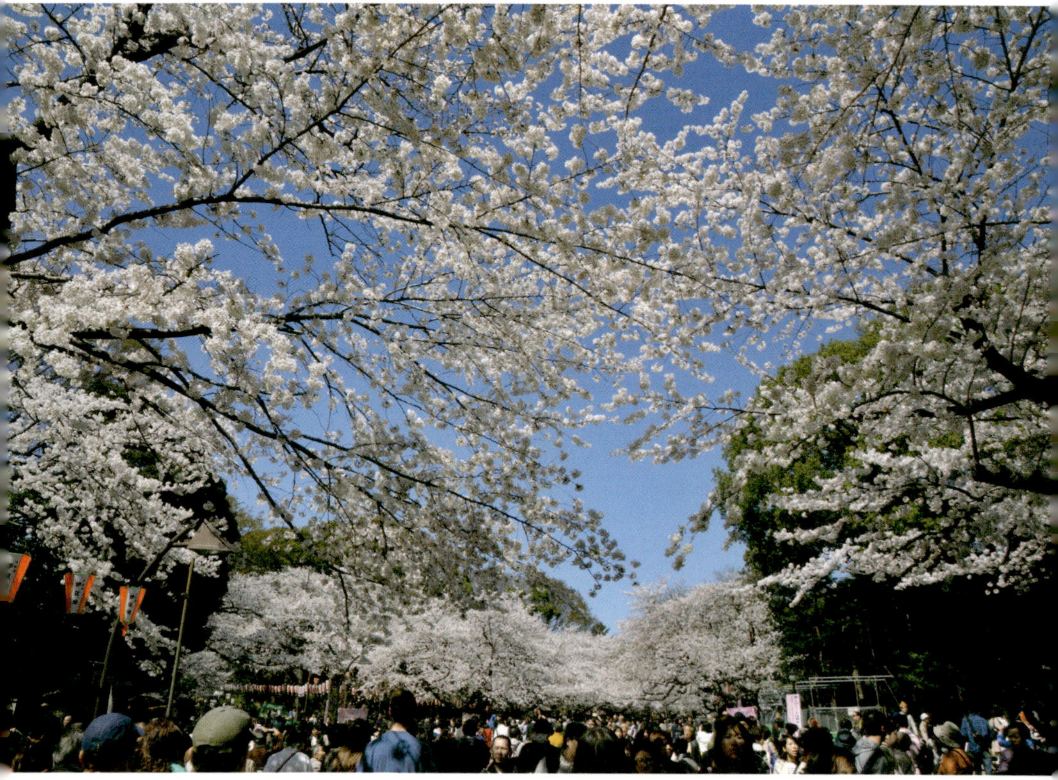

Koinobori こいのぼり

May 5th is today a national holiday called Children's Day. But the traditional names for it are *Tango-no-sekku* (Boys' Festival) or *Shobu-no-sekku* (Iris Festival).

Many insects appear in May and farmers used to erect flowing banners in the fields to drive them off the crops. Big banners bearing family crests were erected at their houses by the samurai class to celebrate the birth of sons. Around the end of the 18th century, not to be outdone, the farmers and merchants decided to create their own displays. They developed paper streamers representing carp swimming upstream against the current—tough, fearless and persistent, but calm when about to die. This was the origin of the *koinobori* carp streamers resembling windsocks that are still erected today by families with sons from around the end of April.

5月5日は今では「こどもの日」と呼ばれる国民の祝日だ。しかし、伝統的な名称は端午の節句もしくは菖蒲の節句である。

5月にはたくさんの昆虫が姿を現すため、農家の人々は田畑に風にたなびく旗を立て、作物から虫たちを追い払う習慣があった。家紋のついた大きなのぼりは、侍階級の人々が、息子の誕生を祝うために屋敷に立てた。18世紀末ごろになると、ひけをとるまいと、農家や商家の人々が自分たち独自の飾り物をつくるようになった。彼らは、コイが川の流れに逆らって上流へと登っていく姿を象徴する紙の飾りリボンをつくった。流れに立ち向かうコイのたくましさ、勇敢さ、根気強さ、そして死に際しての平常心を象徴している。これが円すい状の吹流しに似たこいのぼりの起源で、今日でも男の子のいる家庭では4月末ごろになると、こいのぼりを立てる。

歳時記・春

Gogatsu-ningyo 五月人形

Another traditional Boys' Festival custom that continues today is the display of various items related to male strength and bravery (*gogatsu-ningyo*).

In the old days, a boy's fortune could depend greatly on his skill with weapons. In May, the family's heirlooms of armor, helmets, swords, etc, would be brought out for airing, and the father of the family would lecture his sons on the historic deeds of fighting figures of the past. These ranged from actual warriors, such as Hideyoshi and Yoshitsune, to strong legendary boys, such as Momotaro and Kintaro. Pictures and dolls of these characters would also be displayed.

　今日まで続く伝統的な端午の節句のもう1つの風習は、男の強さと勇敢さにちなんださまざまなものを飾ることだ（五月人形）。
　その昔、男の子の運命は武器を扱う腕前に大きく左右された。5月になると、先祖伝来の家宝の武器であるよろい、かぶと、剣などは、虫干しのために外に出され、一家の父親が、歴史に名を刻んだ過去のつわものたちの功績を息子たちに語って聞かせた。秀吉や義経のように実在した武士から、桃太郎や金太郎のような伝説上のたくましい男の子まで、その人物は広範囲に及んだ。そしてそのようなつわものの絵や人形も、同じように飾られた。

歳時記・春

SUMMER

Tanabata-kazari 七夕飾り

The colorful *Tanabata-no-sekku* (Weaving Loom Festival) was formerly held on the 7th day of the 7th month of the lunar calendar. Today it's held on July 7th in most parts of Japan, or one month later. Also called *Hoshi Matsuri* (Star Festival), it originated around the 8th century. It's based on Chinese stories about celestial lovers who were only allowed to cross the Milky Way to meet once a year. The wife was Orihime, a celestial princess who was a skilled weaver (Vega, the Weaver) and her husband was Hikoboshi (Altair, the Cowherd). Tanabata became a popular festival for all ages during the Edo period. Wishes are written on long colored strips of paper (*tanzaku*), which are hung from a bamboo branch.

　色鮮やかな七夕の節句（機織の祭り）は、以前は太陰暦の第7月の7日目に行われた。現在では、日本のほとんどの地域で7月7日か、その1カ月後に行われる。星祭りとも呼ばれ、8世紀ごろから始まった。1年にたった一度だけ天の川を越えることを許された天空の恋人たちをつづった中国の物語がもとになっている。妻は機織に長けていた織姫（ベガ、織女星）で、夫は彦星（アルタイル、牽牛星）であった。七夕は、江戸時代に世代を問わず人気のあるお祭りになった。細長い色紙（短冊）に願い事を書いて、竹の枝につるす。

141

歳時記・夏

Hanabi 花火

Japanese fireworks (*hanabi*, flower fire) are now regarded as the finest in the world. *Hanabi* are an integral part of Japanese summer festivities, both in the form of massive displays (*hanabi-taikai*) and small personal parties in gardens and streets. To the Japanese, there is something refreshing and even 'cooling' about fireworks on hot, humid summer evenings. Large displays are held nationwide in July and August, many of them above rivers or the sea, where there is a pleasant breeze and beautiful reflections in the water. They feature a great variety of exquisite *uchiage-hanabi*, giant bursts of color, as well as *shikake-hanabi*, set piece fireworks with special effects.

　日本の花火は、今や世界で最も優れたものとされている。花火は日本の夏の祭典になくてはならないもので、それは大規模な花火大会でも、庭や通りで楽しむささやかなパーティーでも、どちらでも同じだ。日本人にとって、蒸し暑い夏の夜の花火はすがすがしく、「涼しく」さえしてくれるものなのである。大規模な大会は全国的に7月から8月にかけて開催され、その多くはさわやかな風があって水面に映る花火が美しい河川敷や海辺で行われる。とりどりの色がパッと大きく開く多様で絶妙な打ち上げ花火だけでなく、特別な仕掛けが施された仕掛花火が呼び物になる。

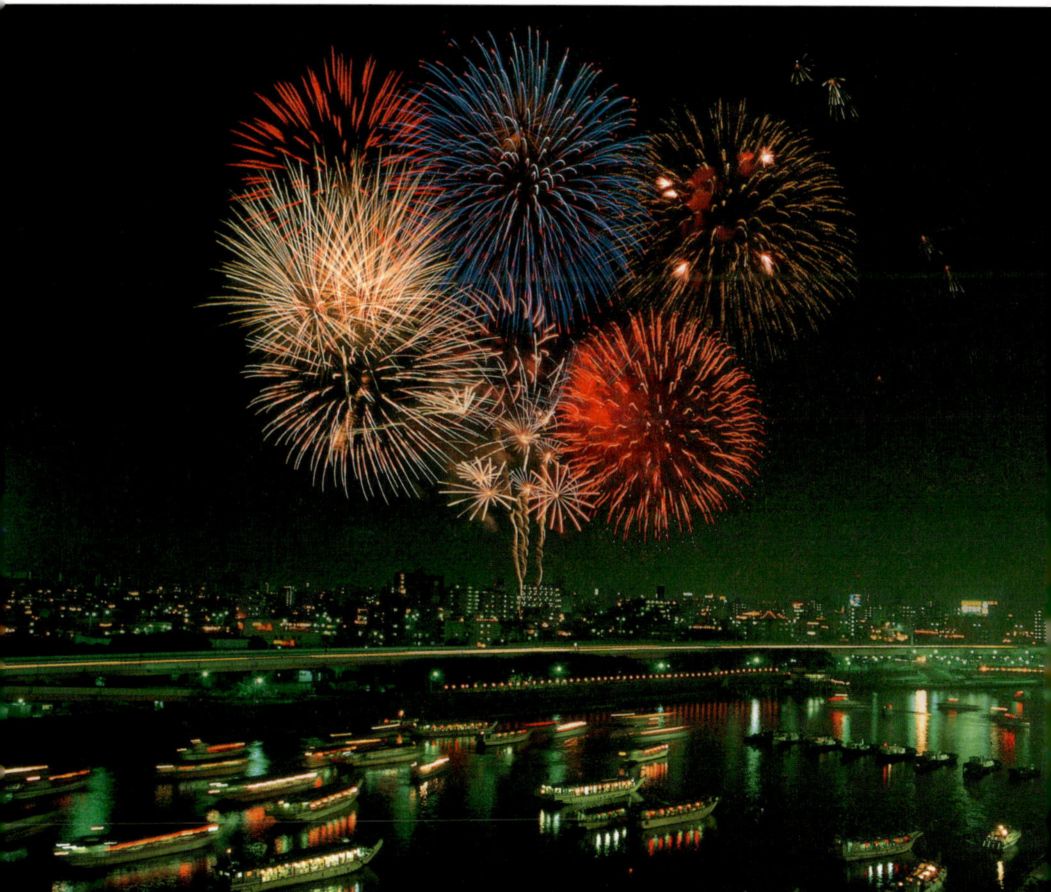

Mikoshi 神輿

Intricately carved *mikoshi* (deity palanquin) portable shrines play a major role in festivals for taking the local god on a tour of the neighborhood to give a divine blessing. They can weigh up to several tons and need hundreds of men and, increasingly, women to carry them on wooden poles, a joint effort mirroring the traditional communal work in fields. The shaking movements are said to reflect the power of the enshrined deity, not just the enthusiasm and inebriation of the bearers.

The mikoshi are usually made of wood with black lacquer and gilding. They are rather like small shrine buildings, with miniature *torii* gates, steps, and a complex roof topped by a gold phoenix (*hoo*). Other mikoshi are tiny and pulled along on carts by children.

きめ細かい彫刻を施された神輿が、さまざまな祭りで中心的な役割を果たす。ご加護を与える氏神さまを乗せて近隣を巡行するのである。重量が数千キロになるものもあり、何百人もの男性の力が必要だ。最近では女性のかつぎ手も増えている。この結束力は、農作業で必要とされていた共同労働の姿を映し出すかのようだ。神輿を上げ下げする動作は鎮座する神の力を反映しているのであって、単にかつぎ手たちの熱狂や酩酊によるものではないとされている。

神輿はたいてい木製で黒漆や金箔が施されている。神社を小さくした感じで、ミニチュアの鳥居、階段、入り組んだ屋根などからなり、屋根の上には金色の不死鳥（鳳凰）が乗っている。他に小型で子供たちが台車で引っ張る神輿もある。

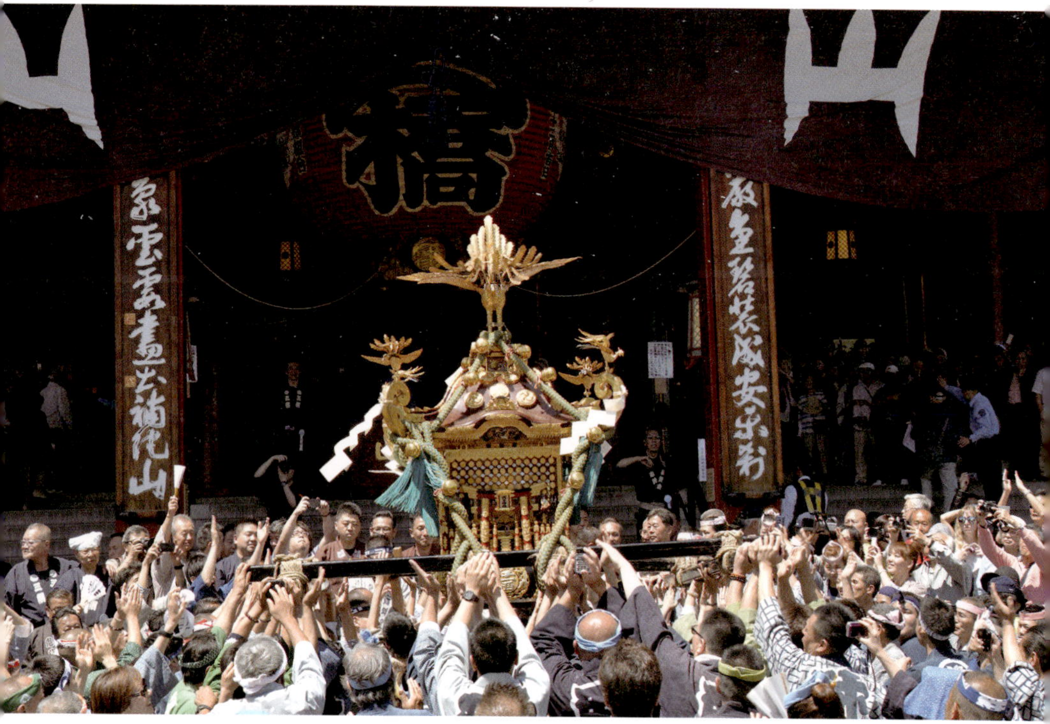

Bon-kazari 盆飾り

The three-day *O-Bon* (or *Urabon-e*) festival in July or August welcomes back the spirits of the dead for their annual visit. Basically a Buddhist festival, but also connected with Shinto ancestor worship, it's a mixture of fond memories and ancestor respect with lively communal events such as *Bon-odori* dances. *Bon-chochin* lanterns are set up in the house and small offerings of the spirits' favorite food are made on a *shoryo-dana* (spirit altar). In some places, floating lanterns are released in the river to send off the spirits (*toro-nagashi* or *shoryo-nagashi*).

　お盆(または盂蘭盆会)は、7月または8月の3晩に、年に一度訪れる祖先の精霊を迎えるために行われる。神道の祖先崇拝と関係の深い仏教行事である。故人をしのび、盆踊りなど地元主催の楽しいイベントで祖先に敬意を表す。家の中に提灯を置き(盆提灯)、特別に精霊を迎えるための棚(精霊棚)を設け、故人の好物だった食べ物を供える。場所によっては、提灯を川に浮かべ海へと流し先祖の霊を送る(灯籠流し、または精霊流し)。

歳時記・夏

Sensu 扇子

Fans have long been connected with the decorative and performing arts as well as daily life. It's said that the first Chinese fans in Japan did not fold. The Japanese claim to have invented *sensu* folding fans more than a thousand years ago, based on a study of the wings of bats. Since then they have acquired many different functions as well as being a canvas for all kinds of paintings and calligraphy and an intrinsic part of theater performances, *rakugo* storytelling, *buyo* Japanese dance, and the tea ceremony. The basic structure of a *sensu* is up to 25 bamboo ribs covered with folded *washi* paper. Some are made entirely of scented wood or use silk instead of paper.

扇子は日常生活で使われてきたが、装飾芸術とも舞台芸術ともつながりがある。日本に初めて持ち込まれた中国の扇子は折りたたみ式ではなかったそうだ。日本人は、コウモリの翼を研究して千年以上も前に折りたたみ式の扇子を発明したのだと公言している。以来、扇子は、さまざまな絵や墨文字を描くキャンバスとしてだけでなく、舞台公演や落語、日本舞踊、お茶会などの不可欠な要素としてたくさんの役割を果たしてきた。扇子は、基本的に最大で25本の竹の骨をたたんだ和紙で覆ってつくる。すべて香木でつくられたものや、紙の代わりに絹を用いた扇子もある。

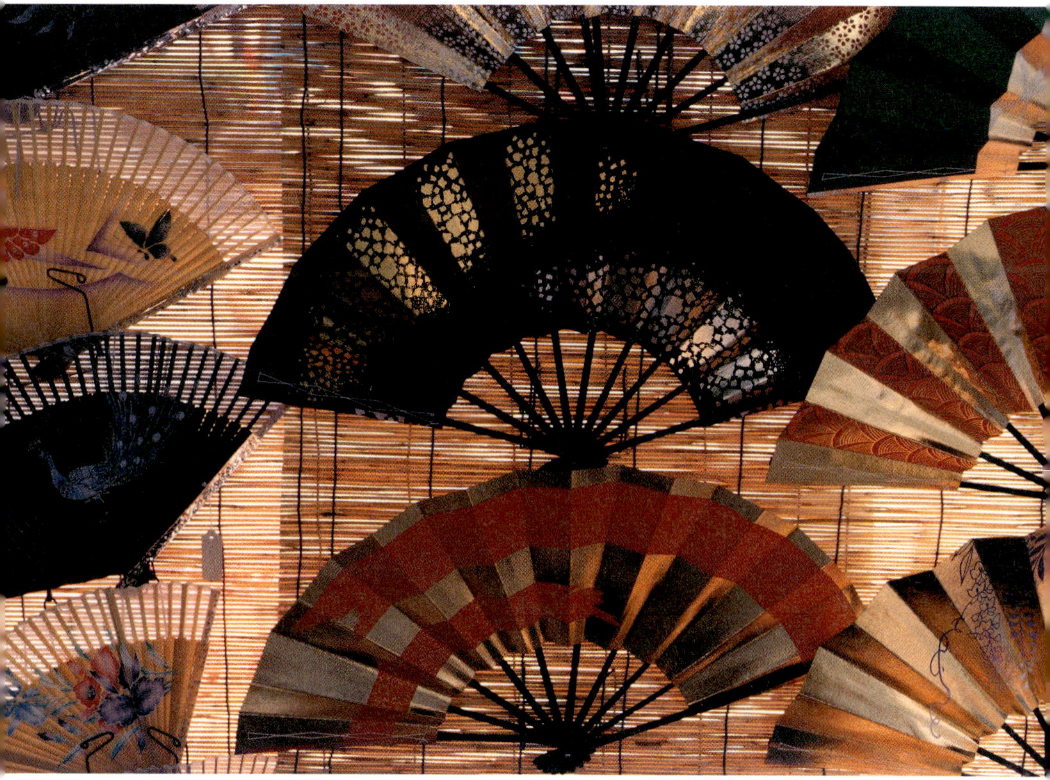

Uchiwa　うちわ

Flat, often circular, fans are called *uchiwa*. They have long been used for advertising purposes, and plastic-ribbed versions are commonly handed out at station exits in summer. Uchiwa come in very handy to stick down the back of a *yukata* (summer kimono) belt. They can also be used like bellows for barbecues and for cooling ingredients such as sushi rice or boiled vegetables. Sumo referees hold a wooden version of the iron *gunbai-uchiwa* once used for giving commands by war commanders.

平たくて丸形が多い扇はうちわと呼ばれる。うちわは長い間広告媒体として使われていて、夏にはプラスチックの骨でつくったものを駅の出口で配っているシーンによく出くわす。うちわは浴衣（夏の着物）の帯の後ろに簡単に差し込める。またバーベキューのときにはふいごのように使ったり、すしめしやゆでた野菜など食材を冷ますときにも使うことができる。相撲の行司は、かつて合戦で大将が指揮をとるのに用いた鉄製の軍配団扇の木製版を使っている。

歳時記・夏

Sudare & Yoshizu　すだれ／よしず

In the days before air-conditioning and electric fans, the Japanese devised various types of blinds and screens to keep their houses cool in the fierce heat of the sun, provide some kind of breeze, and cut out direct sunlight. The general name for bamboo blinds is *sudare* and reed screens are called *yoshizu*. The ideal materials are not affected by humidity and are preferably grown in Japan, because they tend to be more resistant to mold than imported materials.

　エアコンや扇風機が普及する前、日本人は太陽の強烈な熱から家を涼しくしておくために、風を通しつつ、直射日光を避けるためのさまざまな日除けやついたてを考案した。竹製の日除けの一般名は「すだれ」、アシのついたては「よしず」と呼ばれる。材料としては湿気に強く、できれば日本で育ったものが理想的とされている。というのも、輸入ものよりもカビに強い傾向にあるからだ。

歳時記・夏

Kakigori　かき氷

Ice was once a rare commodity, only available to the aristocracy who could pay for its transport from northern mountain areas. Japanese travelers overseas in the late 19th century discovered ice cream. It soon became possible to produce ice and one of today's favorite Japanese summer treats—*kakigori* (shaved ice).

　Wherever you go in summer, you will see small red, white and blue flags bearing the character for 'ice.' This usually means that ice-cream and kakigori are on sale. You will find it at convenience stores (sometimes ready packed), on beaches, and at festivals, and many people make their own at home.

　かつて氷はめったに手に入らないもので、北の山間部からの運送代をまかなえた貴族だけが手に入れることができた。19世紀後半に海外を旅した日本人がアイスクリームというものを発見した。まもなく氷の製造が可能となり、今日、日本人のお気に入りの夏の食べ物の1つであるかき氷（削った氷）もつくられるようになった。

　夏になると、どこへ行っても「氷」と書かれた赤、白、青の旗が目に入る。これはアイスクリームやかき氷を売っているというしるしである。かき氷はコンビニ（すでにパッケージに入っていることもある）や、ビーチや、祭りでも目にする。また、自宅でかき氷をつくる人も多い。

歳時記・夏

Kaya　蚊帳

At one time mosquito nets (*kaya*) were an essential part of daily life. Square in shape, they were hung by four corners from the ceiling and fixed to pegs on the floor, filling most of the room. There were smaller versions with a bamboo frame for young children. Kaya have gradually become unnecessary thanks to improved construction methods, better fitting windows and doors, the introduction of air-conditioning, and the sliding metal-framed *amido* (mosquito-netting doors) that run on rails outside windows. However, kaya made of hemp or polyester that hang loose to the floor can still be bought for use in old houses or for camping.

　かつて、蚊帳は日常生活に欠かせないものだった。四角い形で、4隅を天井からつるし、留めくぎで床に固定して部屋のほとんどを覆った。子供には竹枠つきの小さめのものを使った。建築技術の改善や、しっかり閉まるようになった窓や戸、エアコンの普及、そして外の窓枠にとりつける金属製の引き戸式網戸の普及により、多くの人にとって、蚊帳の必要性はしだいになくなってきた。しかし、麻やポリエステルでつくられた床に固定しないタイプの蚊帳は今でも販売されており、古い家やキャンプ用に使うことが可能だ。

歳時記・夏

Katori-senko　蚊取り線香

If you want to keep the doors and windows open in summer or sit outside, then it's advisable to use some sort of mosquito repellent. The traditional style called *katori-senko* consists of slow-burning coils of hard green incense made from pyrethrum chrysanthemum petals. They usually come in a tin with a short metal stand to hold the coil in the air as it burns, and last for about 10 hours. Earthenware containers shaped like a fat pig have long been popular for holding the coils. There are modern electric versions for use in closed rooms that exude insect-killing fumes from small mats or liquid, and various miniature portable mosquito-repellent devices, including wristbands and ultrasonic keyholders.

夏に戸や窓を開けておきたい場合や屋外にいたい場合は、何らかの虫除けを使うことをすすめる。蚊取り線香と呼ばれる昔ながらの虫除けは、除虫菊の花びらからつくられた固い緑の香をコイル状に巻きつけたもので、ゆっくり燃える。たいていは缶に入っていて、コイルが燃える間、支えておくための金属のスタンドがついている。蚊取り線香は10時間くらいもつ。丸々としたブタの形をした陶器製の容器はコイル立てとして昔から親しまれている。締め切った部屋には小さなマットや液体から虫を殺す香りが出る近代的な電気蚊取り線香、またリストバンドや超音波のキーホルダーなど、持ち運び可能なミニチュアの蚊除け装置がある。

歳時記・夏

Furin　風鈴

There are many traditional ways to help the mind and body forget the heat and humidity of mid-summer in Japan, including lots of chilling ghost stories on TV and the Kabuki stage. Another charming and inexpensive way is to hang a small *furin* wind-bell from the eaves of the house or an adjacent tree. The tinkling noise, created by a puff of breeze, somehow helps you feel a little cooler. Dating back to the 14th century, furin can be made of glass, porcelain, bamboo or metal. Attached to the clapper is something to catch the wind—usually a long piece of paper, or even a feather.

　日本の真夏の蒸し暑さを心身ともに忘れさせてくれる方法はたくさんあって、テレビや歌舞伎の舞台での、背筋が寒くなるような怪談話などもそうである。もう1つの魅力的で安上がりな方法としては、家の軒下や近くの木に小さな風鈴をつるすことだ。一陣の風が吹くとチリンチリンという音が鳴り、なんとなしに涼しい気分にしてくれる。14世紀ごろから使われ始めた風鈴は、ガラスや磁器、竹や金属からつくられる。鈴の舌につけるのは風を受け止めるもので、たいていは1枚の長い紙だが、羽をつけることもある。

歳時記・夏

AUTUMN

Momiji-gari 紅葉狩り

Much of Japan is mountainous and forested, and there are large numbers of deciduous broadleaved trees that change color in autumn, especially *momiji* (maples) which turn red and *icho* (gingkoes) which turn yellow. The Japanese have long loved the beauty of the autumn colors (*koyo*). In the Heian period in the 11th century, aristocrats would gather to view them and write appreciative but wistful poems. This was known as *momiji-gari* (maple hunting) and it spread to the common people from around the 16th century. The roads leading to famous momiji-gari locations, such as Nikko in Tochigi Prefecture, feature major traffic jams in October and November as everyone hunts for the best views.

日本は国の多くが山林であり、特に赤くなる紅葉（もみじ）や黄色に変わる銀杏（いちょう）など、秋に色づく落葉広葉樹が大量に生育している。日本人は昔から紅葉の美しさを愛でてきた。11世紀の平安時代、公家たちは集まって紅葉を鑑賞し、楽しみながら哀愁をおびた歌をつくったりした。この慣習は紅葉狩りとして知られ、16世紀ごろには一般人にも広がるようになった。栃木県の日光など紅葉狩りの場所として有名な場所に続く道路は、10月や11月になるとベストな眺めを求める人たちで交通渋滞が起こる。

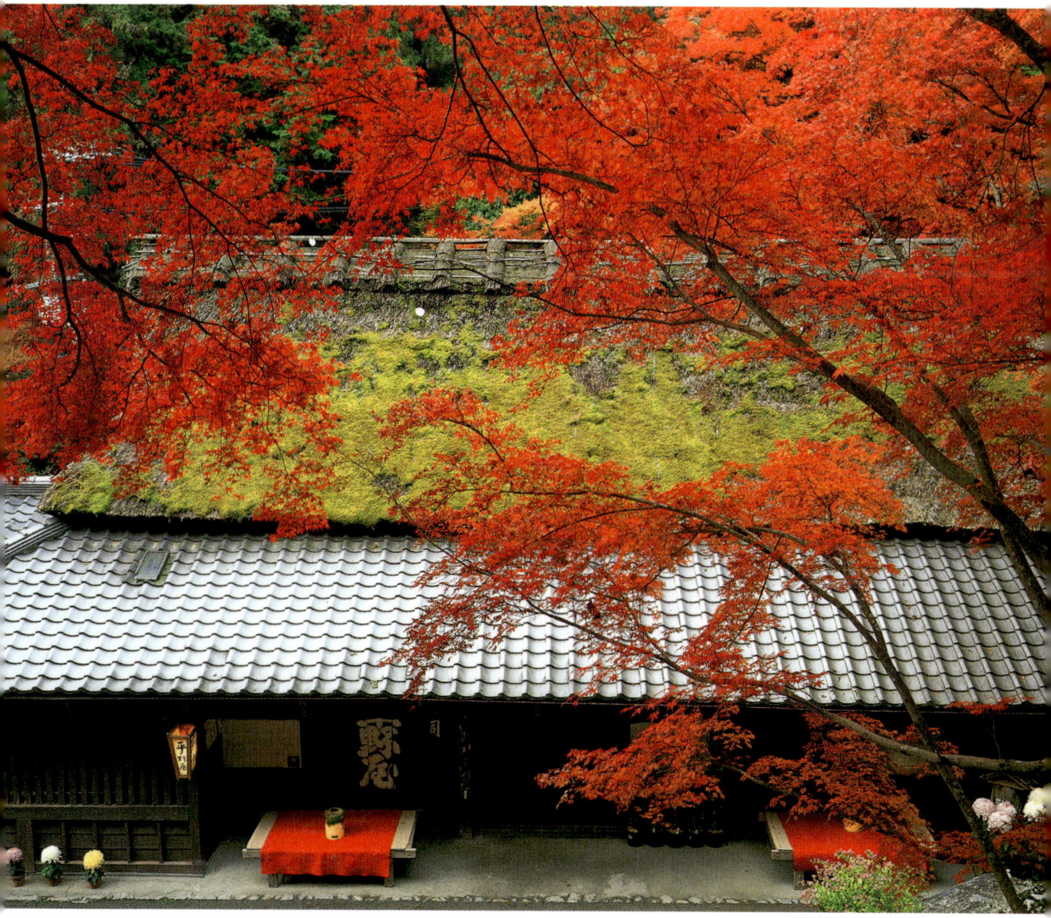

Tsukimi 月見

In Japan, a full moon has no connection with lunacy or werewolves, but only with peace and beauty. In the past, *tsukimi* (moon-viewing) parties were held on *Jugoya* (15th Night of the 8th Month) and *Jusanya* (13th Night of the 9th Month) according to the old lunar calendar. Guests would write moon-related poems while eating and drinking. Tsukimi are still held on the evenings of a full harvest moon (*chushu no meigetsu*) in September and October.

A *sanpo* offering tray is placed on a table facing the direction the moon will appear with items offered to the Moon Goddess. They include a vase of *susuki* (pampas grass) stalks, two flasks of sake, *tsukimi-dango* (rice-flour dumplings), and two candles. There will also be assorted seasonal fruits and vegetables, such as *kaki* (persimmons), *edamame* (boiled soybeans), *kuri* (chestnuts) and *satoimo* (taro).

日本では、満月は狂気や狼男とは何の関係もなく、もっぱら平和と美を象徴するものである。昔は旧暦の十五夜（8番目の月の夜）と十三夜（9番目の月の夜）に月見（月を眺める宴）が行われ、客人は飲食しながら月にまつわる短歌を詠んだ。月見は今でも9月と10月の収穫期の満月（中秋の名月）の夜に催されている。

月が出る方角にテーブルを用意し、その上に三方（さんぽう）という供物台を置く。月の女神へ捧げるのはススキを活けた花瓶と、酒瓶が2本、月見団子、ろうそく2本、そして柿やゆでた枝豆、栗やサトイモなど、季節の果物と野菜を盛り合わせたものである。

歳時記・秋

Shichi-go-san 七五三

The charming and colorful family festival called *Shichi-go-san* (7-5-3) is held at major shrines nationwide in November. Girls (and sometimes boys) aged three, boys aged five, and girls aged seven are dressed up in their finest clothes (*haregi*) and taken to the shrine to pray for good health and a long life. There is a short purification ceremony and a priest reads out the children's names to the deity to give thanks and ask for protection. It's derived from ancient customs in samurai and merchant families to help children survive childhood: from three they could grow their hair, and girls had it tied up (*kamioki*); boys would wear a *hakama* (pleated skirt) from five (*hakamagi*); and girls would wear a proper *obi* (sash) when they were seven (*obitoki* or *himo-otoshi*).

七五三という名の色彩に富んだ楽しい家庭関連の行事が、全国の主な神社で11月に行われる。3歳の女の子（時に男の子もあり）、5歳の男の子、そして7歳の女の子が一張羅の服（晴れ着）を着て、健康と長寿を祈るために神社を詣でるならわしである。簡単なお清めの儀式があり、神職が子どもたちの名前を読み上げ、神道の神々に子供の健康を感謝し長寿を願う。これは、侍や商人の家庭で、その子供たちが幼年期を生き延びるよう願った慣習に由来するものだ。例えば、3歳になると髪を伸ばすことが許され、女の子は髪を結んだり（髪置き）、男の子は5歳で初めて袴（ひだ付きスカート）を身につけ（袴着）、また女の子は7歳になると正式の帯を着用したのである（帯解き、またはひも落とし）。

歳時記・秋

Chitose-ame 千歳飴

After the 7-5-3 ceremony, the children are given long paper bags (*kesho-bukuro*) contained long red and white sticks of *chitose-ame* (1,000-year candy) made from boiled *mizu-ame* (thick malt syrup). The bags are colorfully decorated with many old symbols of long life and good fortune: pine trees, bamboo and plum blossom (together known as *sho-chiku-bai*), cranes, turtles, *noshi*, the sun's rays, Daikoku's lucky hammer, *daruma*, coral, dice, and maybe a picture of Kintaro, the strong boy from old folk tales.

　七五三の儀式が終わると、子供たちには、水あめを煮てつくった長い紅白の棒状の千歳あめが入った縦長の化粧袋が渡される。紙袋には、昔から長寿と幸運の象徴である松竹梅、鶴亀、のし、日光、大黒さんの打出の小づち、だるま、サンゴ、さいころ、そしてときには古い民話に登場する強い男の子、金太郎の絵などが描かれている。

歳時記・秋

Botamochi & Ohagi ぼたもち(おはぎ)

Special rice cakes are prepared for both the spring equinox (*Haru-no-higan*) and the autumn equinox (*Aki-no-higan*). They have different names because of their resemblance to seasonal flowers: *botamochi* (*botan*=peony) in spring and *ohagi* (*hagi*=bush clover) in autumn. They're made from a mixture of steamed rice and *mochigome* (glutinous rice). The ground rice is formed into egg-shaped rice cakes that are covered with red *an* (*azuki* bean paste). A coating of *kinako* (soybean flour) or *kuro-goma* (black sesame) is often added.

春分(春の彼岸)と秋分(秋の彼岸)のいずれにも特別なもちが用意される。それぞれ季節の花に似ているところから異なった名前がつけられている。ぼたもち(牡丹)は春、おはぎ(ハギ)は秋である。蒸した米ともち米を混ぜ合わせてつくる。ついた米をあん(ペースト状の小豆)でくるみ、卵型のもちにしたものだ。きな粉(大豆の粉)や黒ごまをまぶすことがしばしばある。

歳時記・秋

冬 WINTER
Kadomatsu 門松

Christmas decorations disappear in Japan as soon as December 25th comes round because there are so many traditional New Year decorations. An important one placed outside private houses and shops is the *kadomatsu* (gate pine). It represents a landmark to welcome the god of the next year (*toshigami*). Pine branches are used because they are strong and evergreen, suggesting longevity. Ideally, there should be a kadomatsu display on both sides of the entrance: one with a smooth branch of pine (=female); and one with a rough branch with the bark left on (=male).

In its simplest form, the kadomatsu is just a pine branch fixed to the side of the front door. But a full display consists of several important elements that symbolize a long and prosperous life. For example, stalks of bamboo, diagonally sliced at the top like spears symbolize virtue, constancy, and rapid, healthy growth. *Habotan* (ornamental kale) is often included to add some color.

日本では12月25日になったとたんクリスマスの飾りを見なくなる。数多くの伝統的な新年の飾りがこれにとって代わるからだ。一つの重要な飾りは個人宅や商店の入り口あたりに見かける門松(門の松)だ。門松は新しい年の神(年神)を迎える目印で、長寿を意味する強い常緑樹である松の枝を使う。門の右と左の両側に飾るのが理想的とされている。一方にはすべすべした松の枝(女)を飾った門松を、もう一方には樹皮を残したざらざらした枝(男)を飾った門松を立てる。

最もシンプルな飾り方として、松の枝を1本だけ、玄関のドアの端にとめつけるというのがある。しかし正式な飾りつけは、長寿と繁栄を象徴するいくつかの重要な要素で構成されている。例えば、やりのように先端を斜めに切った3本の青竹は、美徳、不変性、速やかで健やかな成長を表している。葉ボタン（装飾用のキャベツ）を、色を添えるために使うことが多い。

Shime-kazari　しめ飾り

Shime-kazari is the term for the New Year decorations full of symbolism that are hung in various places, such as over the entrance to a house. The shime-kazari indicate to the god of the New Year (*toshigami*) that a temporary abode has been created and purified. The base of the decoration is a version of the *shimenawa* twisted sacred ropes seen at Shinto shrines, which symbolize purity. Other common elements are also used in *kagami-mochi* displays inside the house, such as fern fronds (*urajiro*) and dried kelp (*konbu*).

　しめ飾りとは、象徴的な意味がたくさん込められた新年の飾りつけを指す言葉で、玄関の軒先などあちこちに飾られる。しめ飾りは、新年の神（年神）の仮の住まいがつくられ、清められたことを示す。しめ飾りの母体になるのは、神社で見かける清浄を象徴するしめ縄だ。ほかに、裏白（うらじろ）や昆布などの共通要素が、家の中に飾る鏡もちの飾りつけにも使用される。

歳時記・冬

Mochitsuki もちつき

Shortly before the end of the year, many people enjoy pounding hot boiled glutinous rice for making *mochi* rice cakes, an essential element of New Year cuisine. This tradition is called *mochitsuki*.

The old way—claimed to produce the most delicious mochi—is to use a large mortar (*usu*) and a heavy, long-handled wooden mallet (*kine*). The mortars are around one meter high and made of a solid piece of wood or stone hollowed out in the center. Unlike the smaller *suribachi* kitchen mortars, they're smooth inside. The mallet is slammed down on to the dough with an over-the-shoulder action, like chopping wood with an axe. This is done rhythmically, with another person adding water by hand and turning the dough between each blow. It's an exhausting and dangerous operation: a mistimed blow can smash the helper's hand.

　年末近くなると、人々の多くが炊きたてで熱々のもち米をつき、新年の料理に欠かせないもちをつくる。このしきたりはもちつきと呼ばれる。
　一番おいしいもちをつくる方法といわれる古くからのやり方は、大きなうすと重くて柄の長い木製のきねを使うこと。うすは高さが1メートルほどで、たいていケヤキだが、固い木や石の真ん中をくり抜いてつくられる。台所で使われる小型のすり鉢と違い、うすは内側がつるつるしている。きねは、おのでたきぎを割るような動きで、肩の上からもち米のかたまりをバシッとたたくように振り下ろす。もう1人が、きねが振り下ろされる間げきをぬって手水を加えたりもち米のかたまりをひっくり返す。この動作をリズミカルに行うわけだが、体力のいる危険な作業だ。きねを振り下ろすタイミングが乱れると、もちを返す人の手をたたきつぶす可能性もある。

歳時記・冬

Kagami-mochi 鏡もち

Mochi rice balls are a major celebratory feature of New Year cuisine because the sound of 'mochi' suggests another word meaning 'long-lasting.' They're not only displayed but also eaten in various ways. When it became normal to construct *tokonoma* alcoves in houses in the Muromachi Period (1336–1573), the custom began of displaying mochi in them as an *osonae* (offering to the unseen) and a prayer for good fortune.

Today, two round *kagami-mochi* (mirror rice-cakes) with flat bottoms are placed on top of each other on a plain wooden *sanpo* stand. The display usually includes some *konbu* (kelp), a *daidai* (bitter orange) or a *mikan* (mandarin), *urajiro* (fern leaves), and a skewer of dried *kaki* (persimmons). A ceremony called *kagami-biraki* (opening the mirror) is held on January 11th to break up the hardened rice balls and eat them.

もちは、お正月に食べる料理の中でもひときわめでたい意味合いを持つ。というのも「もち」という言葉の響きが「永く続く」という意味を連想させるからだ。もちは飾るだけでなく、さまざまな調理法で食される。室町時代（1336～1573）、家に床の間をつくるのが一般的になると、お供え（見えざる存在への捧げ物）として、また幸運を祈って、床の間にもちを飾る習慣が始まった。

現代では、木製の三方（さんぽ）という供物台に円くて平たい鏡もちを2つ重ねて置く。これに、何枚かの昆布とダイダイあるいはミカン、シダの葉である裏白、串にさした干し柿を飾るのが一般的だ。1月11日に行われる鏡開きと呼ばれる儀式では、その日まで飾られて硬くなったもちを割って食べる。

歳時記・冬

Toshikoshi-soba 年越しそば

December 31st, which launches the start of the important New Year celebrations, is called *omisoka*. It's a custom for families to eat hot buckwheat noodles (*toshikoshi-soba*) in the evening before midnight (but not after). The name literally means 'year-crossing noodles'—in other words, seeing out the old year and welcoming in the new. Various reasons are given for this custom. One common explanation is that the length of soba noodles symbolizes longevity. Another is that soba is easy to cut, so it symbolizes the cutting off of all the hardships, troubles and debts of the year just ending.

　12月31日は、大切な新年の祝賀が始まろうとするときで、大みそかと呼ばれる。夜中の12時までに(後ではいけない)、熱々のそば(年越しそば)を家族で食べるならわしがある。文字どおり「年を越す麺」であり、言い換えると、古き年を見送り新しい年を迎える意味を持つ。このならわしについては諸説ある。広く知られているのは、そばの長さが長寿を象徴しているという説だ。そばが切れやすいことから、終わろうとしているその年の苦難や不幸、借金などすべてひっくるめて断ち切ることを象徴するとの説もある。

歳時記・冬

Joya-no-kane 除夜の鐘

Japanese temple bells are rung 108 times (*joya-no-kane*) on New Year's Eve or early on January 1st. This represents driving away the 108 sins of the world and starting the new year fresh and pure. In the old days, the 108th ring would coincide with midnight. However, in recent years a Western-style 'countdown' to midnight has even spread to some major temples, and the first ring marks midnight. At many temples, it's possible to apply in advance to be one of the bell-ringers for a small contribution.

日本の寺院では、大みそかの深夜か元旦の早朝に108つの鐘をつく（除夜の鐘）。鐘を108回つくのは、俗世の108の煩悩を追い払い、新年を新鮮で純粋な気分で始めるという意味がある。昔は108回目の鐘は午前0時ぴったりに鳴らされたものだったが、最近では午前0時まで「カウントダウン」する西洋スタイルがいくつかの大きな寺院に広まり、最初の鐘が午前0時を刻むようになった。あらかじめ少額のお布施をして申し込んでおけば、鐘を1回つかせてくれる寺院も多い。

歳時記・冬

Hatsu-mode 初詣

The first visit of the year to a temple or shrine is called *hatsu-mode*. Some people like to combine it with the countdown to midnight on December 31st. Others prefer to see the New Year in at home and then head out, or go during one of the first three days of January, which are called *san-ga-nichi*. Only January 1st is a national holiday, but many people take at least three days' holiday. In the case of major shrines such as Tsurugaoka Hachimangu in Kamakura and Meiji Jingu in Tokyo, several million people visit during this period every year. Progress toward the main buildings is extremely slow! Huge *saisenbako* money boxes are prepared so that visitors can throw money and then pray for a successful year.

年が明けて初めて寺院や神社に詣でることを初詣（はつもうで）と呼ぶ。真夜中のカウントダウンと初詣を同時に行おうとする人もいれば、新年を家で迎え、それから初詣に出かける人、あるいは１月の１日から３日までの間に出かける人もいる。この３日間を三が日と呼ぶ。１日だけが国民の祝日だが、少なくとも３日間の休暇をとる人が多い。鎌倉の鶴岡八幡宮や東京の明治神宮といった大きな神社では、毎年この３日間に数百万人が初詣に訪れる。本殿に向かう列は遅々として進まない！寺院や神社には大きな賽銭箱が設けてあり、初詣客が現金を投げ入れ、よい年になるよう祈願できるようになっている。

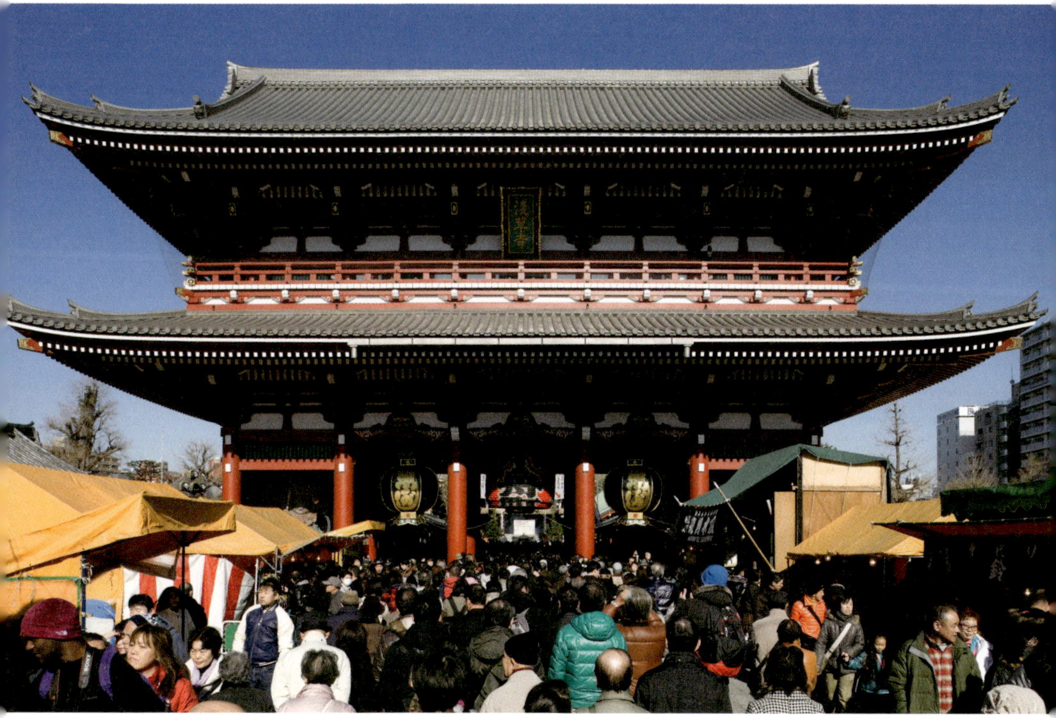

Hamaya　破魔矢

One of the most popular lucky charms on sale at shrines at the New Year are wooden arrows called *hamaya*. Said to be swift and sure carriers of good fortune that help to preserve a house or business against evil and all kinds of calamity during the coming year, they are usually kept in a high position above a doorway or window. Generally around 60 centimeters long, they have white synthetic feathers, but not a sharp tip. Red, white, gold or silver paper is wrapped around the shaft, bearing the shrine's name. There may also be small bells and an *ema* votive tablet attached. The idea is to buy a new *hamaya* every year and take the one from the previous year for burning at the shrine it came from.

新年に神社で販売されている最も人気のあるお守りの1つに、破魔矢と呼ばれる木製の矢がある。破魔矢は速やかに、また確実に幸運をもたらし、来たる年に家や商売を不運やあらゆる災難から守るといわれているが、通常、戸口や窓の上の高いところに飾っておく。一般に長さは60センチほどで、白い合成の羽がついているが、先は尖っていない。矢の柄には神社の名前が書かれた赤、白、金、あるいは銀色などの紙を巻いてあったり、小さな鈴や奉納額である絵馬がついていることもある。毎年新しいものを買い、前年のものは買った神社で焼いてもらうのがならわしだ。

歳時記・冬

O-toso おとそ

For more than 1,000 years, a special type of sweet sake called *o-toso* (defeat evil) has been drunk on the morning of January 1st and offered to guests over the holiday period. It's regarded as a protection against sickness and evil. The recipe varies around Japan, but basically consists of sake or *mirin* (sweet cooking sake), spiced with medicinal herbs, including Japanese pepper (*sansho*), ginger, rhubarb, cinnamon and cassia bark. A suitable mixture of herbs used to be given out as a New Year gift from doctors and pharmacies. Today most people buy a ready-prepared teabag of spices to add to some sake on New Year's Eve and leave overnight. It's served into lacquered sake cups (*sakazuki*) from a decorative flask, such as a *kyusu* teapot.

　千年以上にわたって、1月1日の朝には邪気をはらう「おとそ」と呼ばれる甘みのある特殊な酒を飲み、正月中はこれを客にふるまう風習が続いている。おとそは、疫病や厄神から身を守ると考えられている。おとそのつくり方は日本各地でさまざまだが、基本的には、酒あるいはみりん（甘い料理酒）を、山椒、ショウガ、ダイオウ、シナモン、ケイヒなどの薬効のある香草で味つけする。昔は、医者と薬屋が、おとそに合う香草を混ぜたものを新年の贈り物として配る習慣があった。現代ではそうした香辛料がティーバッグになったものを買って、大みそかに酒に加え、ひと晩寝かせるという人がほとんどである。おとそは急須のような華やかな酒瓶から塗りの杯にそそいで供される。

歳時記・冬

O-toshidama お年玉

Gifts of money called *o-toshidama* (year jewels) are a main attraction of the New Year for children. Until the 20th century, Japan had no general tradition of giving individuals birthday or Christmas presents. This custom developed from several ancient practices: families exchanging presents at the New Year; shrines and temples distributing gifts they had themselves received; and the custom of the oldest member of a family representing the god of the New Year (*toshigami*) by presenting to the younger members of the family the *mochi* rice cakes that had been dedicated to the god. Today, relatives and family friends present children with special decorated envelopes (*o-toshidama-bukuro*) containing money.

　お年玉（年の宝）と呼ばれるお金の贈り物は、子供にとって正月一番の楽しみである。20世紀になるまで、日本には誕生日やクリスマスにプレゼントを贈り合うという習慣はなかった。お年玉は古代の風習から発展したものである。たとえば、新年に家族でプレゼントを交換するという風習。あるいは神社や寺院が、受けとった贈り物を配るという風習。そして家族で最年長の者が、新年の神（年神）の代理として、若い者たちに神に供えていたもちを与える風習。現代では、親戚や家族の友人が特別なデザインの封筒（お年玉袋）にお金を入れて子供に贈る。

191

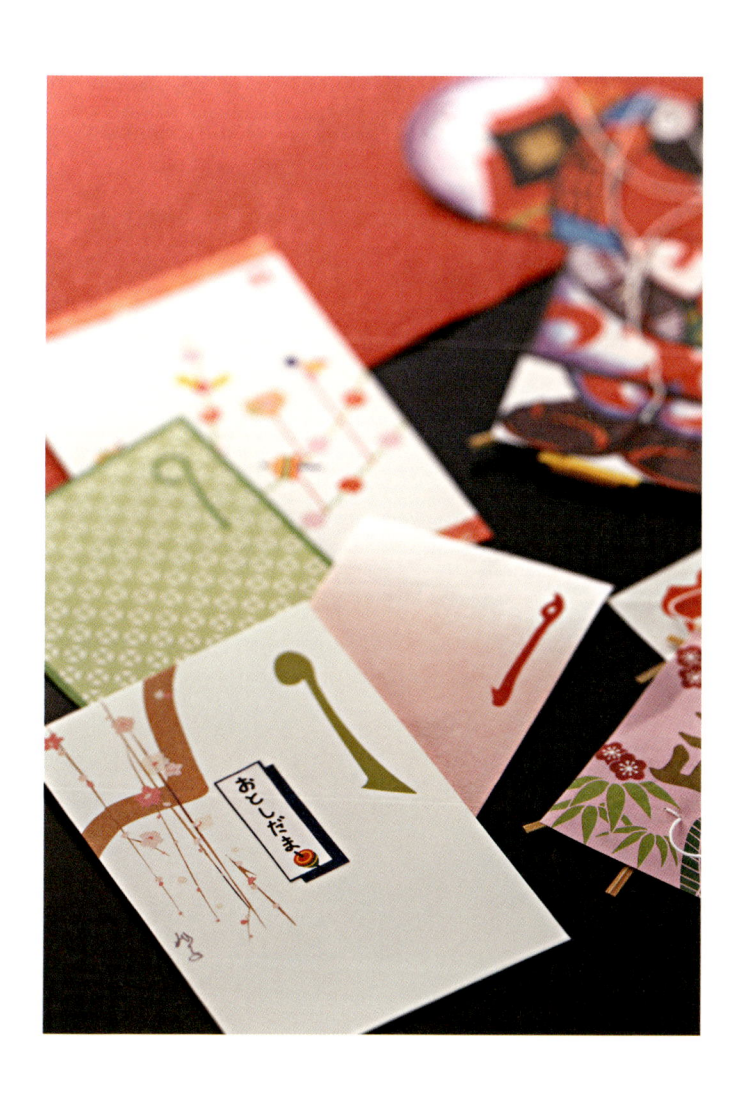

歳時記・冬

O-sechi-ryori おせち料理

Various special food items are served at the New Year, both for the family and guests. One of them is *zoni*, a hot soup containing *mochi*, pieces of chicken, citron peel, etc. Usually a clear soup in the Kanto and Kyushu regions, it's often made with *miso* (fermented soybean paste) in Kansai. The traditional mixture of symbolic seafood, meat, vegetable and pickled dishes is called *o-sechi-ryori*. The items can all be made in advance and eaten cold, giving housewives and househusbands a welcome rest from kitchen work. Only the soup and the rice need to be served hot. However, it's now common to order *o-sechi-ryori* from restaurants or shops, often including non-traditional items such as Chinese dishes or sushi. And some people prefer not to eat the same items for three days!

新年には、家族と来客に特別なごちそうが供される。その1つ、雑煮は新年に食べる温かい汁物で、もちと小さく切った鶏肉、ゆずの皮などが入っている。関東や九州では通常すまし汁、関西では味噌入りでつくられることが多い。それぞれ象徴的な意味を持つ魚介類や肉、野菜、酢の物をとり混ぜた伝統的な料理を、おせち料理という。おせち料理は前もってつくることが可能で、冷えたまま食べられるものばかりなので、主婦や主夫は台所仕事から解放される。温かい汁物とご飯だけを用意すればよいというわけだ。とはいっても、今ではレストランや店におせち料理を注文することはよくあることで、中華料理やすしなど、伝統とは関係のない食べ物が入っていることもしばしばだ。それに3日も続けて同じ料理を食べるのはいやだという人もいる！

193

歳時記・冬

Kamakura　かまくら

In the snowy areas of northern Japan there's a tradition for children to build round *kamakura* snow houses like small igloos. There's room inside for three or four children to sit on cushions on thin straw mats (*mushiro*). Lighting is traditionally provided by candles, but today many are fitted with electric lighting and even a *kotatsu* heated table. However, children still often sit around a small *hibachi* charcoal heater and grill *mochi* rice cakes. A small recess is made in the back wall for a miniature *kamidana* shrine dedicated to Suijin, the God of Water, and prayers are offered for ample spring rain. If the door is covered with a *sudare* screen, it can be quite warm inside and some children even stay in the kamakura overnight.

日本北部の積雪地帯に、子供たちが小さなイグルーのような丸い雪の家、かまくらをつくる伝統がある。中には3～4人の子供がむしろの上に座布団を敷いて座れるくらいのスペースがある。明かりはろうそくだけというのがならわしだったが、今日では電灯を備えたものも多く、こたつが置いてあるものさえある。しかし、子供たちは今でも小さな火鉢を囲んで座り、もちを焼くことが多い。かまくらの奥の壁には小さなくぼみをつくり、水神を祭る小さな神棚を飾って、春に十分な雨が降るようにと祈りを捧げる。入り口にすだれがかかっていると、中はとても暖かく、夜どおしかまくらの中で過ごす子供もいる。

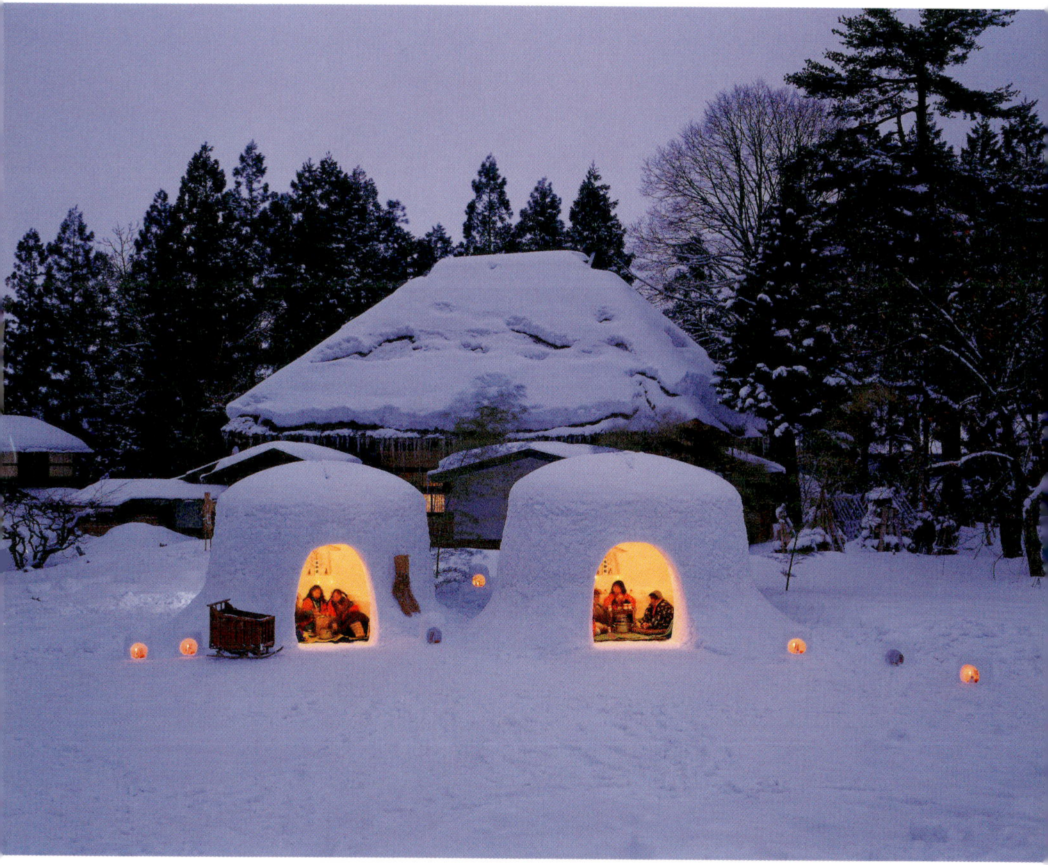

日本風物詩

2014年 7月2日 第1刷発行
2024年 11月2日 第4刷発行

著　者	ステュウット　ヴァーナム−アットキン
訳　者	とよざきようこ
発行者	賀川　洋
発行所	IBCパブリッシング株式会社 〒162-0804 東京都新宿区中里町29番3号 菱秀神楽坂ビル TEL 03-3513-4511 FAX 03-3513-4512 www.ibcpub.co.jp
印刷所	日新印刷株式会社

©2014 Stuart Varnam-Atkin, Yoko Toyozaki

落丁本・乱丁本は小社宛にお送りください。
送料小社負担にてお取り替えいたします。
本書の無断複写（コピー）は
著作権法上での例外を除き禁じられています。

ISBN 978-4-7946-0286-2
Printed in Japan